MW00441371

The Meaning of Faith

& The Sick Are Healed

RESOLVING THE MYSTERIES OF FAITH

DR. CHARLES S. PRICE

© Copyright 2002 – John W. Carver, Jr. and Timothy Enloe

All rights reserved. This book is protected by the copyright laws of the United States of America. This book may not be copied or reprinted for commercial gain or profit. The use of short quotations or occasional page copying for personal or group study is permitted and encouraged. Permission will be granted upon request. Unless otherwise identified, Scripture quotations are from the King James Version of the Bible. Please note that Destiny Image's publishing style capitalizes certain pronouns in Scripture that refer to the Father, Son, and Holy Spirit, and may differ from some Bible publishers' styles.

Take note that the name satan and related names are not capitalized. We choose not to acknowledge him, even to the point of violating grammatical rules.

Compiled by John W. Carver and Tim N. Enloe

Published by MercyPlace Ministries

MercyPlace is a licensed imprint of Destiny Image®, Inc.

Distributed by

Destiny Image® Publishers, Inc.
P.O. Box 310
Shippensburg, PA 17257-0310

ISBN 0-9707919-5-X

For Worldwide Distribution
Printed in the U.S.A.

This book and all other Destiny Image, Revival Press, MercyPlace, Fresh Bread, Destiny Image Fiction, and Treasure House books are available at Christian bookstores and distributors worldwide.

For a U.S. bookstore nearest you, call **1-800-722-6774**.
For more information on foreign distributors, call **717-532-3040**.
Or reach us on the Internet:
www.destinyimage.com

Acknowledgment

Special thanks to Dr. Price's daughter, Marjorie,
for granting John Carver permission to reprint these books.

Contents

Foreword

*S*ince 1969, I have been on a quest to learn all I can about the healing movement that began in the 1890s and continued throughout the 1960s. It has required hours upon hours of research. During my search, one name associated with almost all of the ministers I have interviewed is that of Dr. Charles S. Price. I have discovered that this man's ministry was a hallmark for ministers and their ministries during a very new era—hundreds of healings and miracles were taking place in his ministry on a regular basis. Because of his genuineness, purity, and lack of compromise, Dr. Price's ministry is still a major influence on many ministries today.

Why was Dr. Price's ministry so important? It was because of the demonstration of the power of God in his services. Dr. Price had an anointing to preach and pray for the sick. Miracle healing took place during a time when you hardly ever saw a miracle. The gifts of the word of knowledge and the word of wisdom, discerning of spirits, and prophecy were operating in Dr. Price's meetings in a phenomenal way. God actually used Dr. Price to prophesy concerning the coming revival, and many of his books are prophetically correct for our day.

In 1993, I had the privilege of interviewing Marjorie Price, Dr. Price's daughter. These are some of the things she had to say.

"Dad was adamant about the teaching on the blood of Christ, and without the shedding of blood, there is no remission of sins. He was loyal to the basics, and sometimes, he was criticized a lot because of his boldness to preach on healing and deliverance from torment. He was always firm on that because he said that he had experienced it. God had dealt with him in many ways, and he couldn't deny what he had seen and heard.

"Many in the church world criticized him because of his belief in the doctrine of divine healing in the atonement being for us today. So many people thought that doctrine ended during the days of Christ, that God had established it only for the early church, but it wasn't for us, today. Dad was a firm believer that it was for all of us.

"Conviction was there. People would come up the aisles with tears streaming down their faces. They knew they had to be saved. My father was always very thankful to lift up the name of Jesus, saying that there is no other way—that Jesus was the way, the truth, and the life, and no man cometh to the Father but by Him. He raised the name of Jesus so powerfully that if they hadn't already accepted the Lord as their personal Savior, they became very repentant. People would throw themselves at the altar, acknowledging their sins, and crying out to God for deliverance. I saw wonderful, wonderful changes in the lives of those dear people."

In 1923, Dr. Price began publishing some of his sermons in book form; the first was *The Great Physician*, followed by *The Potter and the Clay*. Afterward in 1926, he began printing *Golden Grain*, a monthly periodical that was distributed all over the world. It contained many of the great sermons that Dr. Price preached in his meetings, and it extended his ministry to the remote corners of the earth.

During an interview, Clifton Erickson (a *Voice of Healing* minister, who became a very dear friend of mine) had this to say pertaining to the "faith" message of Dr. Price.

"Faith is not something you work up. Faith is a gift of God. To be understood, faith must be experienced. God Gives faith. I can go back to the days of Dr. Price. I sat under his ministry. His book, *The Real Faith*, is powerful! It's plain and simple. He explains what real Bible faith is. There were other books written during the time of Dr. Price's ministry that were way out. There were those who taught that you work your faith up within yourself by doing certain things and saying certain things— certain phraseologies, like 'Lord, I believe, I believe, I believe.' You don't work it up that way because you don't have it within you to begin with. It is something that is an impartation by God Almighty into the heart of man. God gives it! If God doesn't give it, you won't have it! God is the author and perfecter of our faith."

Dr. Price stepped into the Pentecostal scene just 15 years after the *Azusa Street* outpouring. This was also just a few years after the establishment of some of the major church denominations and fellowships. During this time, a line was drawn in the sand (and some in concrete) pertaining to the Pentecostal movement and its doctrines—the baptism in the Holy Ghost, divine healing, supernatural manifestations, sanctification, faith, and many prophetic doctrines. Dr. Price became a beacon in a sea of upheaval. He provided a balance in the Pentecostal movement that was being taken in a lot of different directions.

Dr. Price was rejected by many of his peers because of the stand he took in his preaching. Being the man he was, he just continued ministering what God gave him to minister. Unfortunately, this great man of God went home to be with the Lord before he saw the fulfillment of his work and of the prophetic words that God had spoken through him. Most people didn't realize the importance of Dr. Price's ministry until after his death. He is definitely one of the unsung heroes of Pentecost.

Wayne C. Williams, the author of a book on William Jennings Bryan, once said:

"It has been the unhappy lot of most men who seek reform either to be laughed off the stage or die full of disappointment over the failure of their fellowmen to see the thing(s) which they had seen. History is filled with leaders who, too far in advance of their time, were crucified by their own generation and immortalized by succeeding generations." (*William Jennings Bryan* by Wayne C. Williams)

I've had the privilege of interviewing over 25 *Voice of Healing* ministers and their associates. The *Voice of Healing* was a group of ministers who formed an organization so they could work together during the 1940s and 1950s; each ministry involved had signs, wonders, and miracles taking place in their ministry. During these interviews one name seemed to pop up all the time—Dr. Charles S. Price. Gordon Lindsay, A.A. Allen, Clifton Erickson, T.L. Osborn and a host of others said that Dr. Price's ministry helped motivate, stir, and encourage them to do and to be what God wanted them to do and to be.

Concerning Dr. Price, Rev. Gordon Lindsay wrote:

"The ministry of Dr. Charles S. Price is unique in the history of revivals and must be ranked with that of Wesley, Finney, and Moody in its impact upon the church. I personally have a special interest in his work, as I was pastor of a church for three years that came out of his revival.

"The story of how [Dr. Price] was led from modernism into a born-again experience with God is a thrilling one. Under the influence of certain teachers, he was led away from the simplicity of the gospel until, as he said, 'I very soon got to the point where I could explain every religious emotion from the standpoint of psychology.' But these theories all vanished when he came to this glorious experience with God and received the baptism of the Holy Spirit.

"Many outstanding evangelists and ministers were the fruit of the Price campaigns. Lorne Fox, who was healed of an extreme case of Saint Vitus' dance in one of his meetings, is but one example. Only eternity will reveal the final results of these campaigns, the influence of which has gone out like a wave in the boundless sea into ever widening circles. Many will enjoy its blessings without knowing the original source. Truly, the name of Charles S. Price will stand out on the records both in heaven and in earth as a man God greatly used."

Our purpose in reprinting *The Meaning of Faith* and *The Sick Are Healed* in their original text, is that Dr. Price not only influenced his generation, but his words are also powerful enough to influence today's and future generations. He was a great orator. His style of ministry was that of painting a picture with words, and in today's generation pictures speak so much louder than words. Our prayer is that you will come to know the Word of God in a deeper depth than you have ever known it before as you prayerfully read the pages of this book.

Revelation 14:13 says, "And I heard a voice from heaven saying unto me, Write, Blessed are the dead which die in the Lord from henceforth: Yea, saith the Spirit, that they may rest from their labours; *and their works do follow them.*" Dr. Charles S. Price's works have definitely followed him.

John W. Carver

Introduction

A Brief Biography of Dr. Charles Sydney Price (1887-1947)

*T*he great Ice Arena was crowded to capacity. The fire marshall closed the doors. Thousands were standing outside on the cold Canadian evening in 1923. The overly zealous crowd began to scale the building, smashing windows to hear the evangelist, Dr. Charles S. Price. They had read of the healing miracles on the front pages of the Edmonton, Alberta newspapers and now they wanted to witness this power firsthand.

Who would have guessed that just over a year earlier this man was occupying a modernist pulpit? Dr. Price had denied the necessity of personal salvation and ridiculed those who believed in divine healing. He had even opened a public smoking lounge and billiard room in a previous church.

It was, in fact, these liberal beliefs that led him to a fiery woman evangelist's tent meetings. Some of his own Congregational Church members had been drawn in by the message and charisma of Aimee Semple McPherson. They told their pastor of getting "saved" and of cripples walking and the blind seeing.

Dr. Price felt that he needed to visit one of these meetings to correct the error of his congregants. Certain that he would return with ample ammunition, he took an advertisement out in the local paper announcing his Sunday morning message, "Divine Healing Bubble Bursts." With pen and paper in hand he was ready to expose this woman evangelist and her deception.

While attending the McPherson tent meeting, Dr. Price was astonished by the genuine healings and powerful preaching. He was so convicted of his sin that he, bowing his pride, responded to the evangelist's invitation to accept Christ. Instead of the divine healing bubble bursting, the woman evangelist punctured his own modernist theology!

Within a matter of days he had personally experienced the events of the Day of Pentecost. Now born again and baptized in the Holy Spirit, he decided to present to his congregation an alternate sermon than the one advertised a few days prior.

Dr. Price knew that publicly embracing Full Gospel beliefs would mean dismissal from his pulpit, but he preached his newfound salvation in spite of his fears. To his amazement, over 80 people responded to his appeal for salvation!

Soon prayer meetings were started so that others could receive the baptism in the Spirit evidenced by speaking in unlearned tongues. These meetings lasted through the night, and quickly grew from a few hundred to over a thousand in attendance.

It was becoming evident that God was enlarging the scope of Dr. Price's ministry. Through miraculous circumstances he left the pastorate to begin an evangelistic ministry. His first meetings triggered revivals that shook the Pacific Northwest and eventually the nation of Canada. Soon many of the largest auditoriums in North America were filled with those who wanted to hear his preaching and see miracles.

Dr. Price's ministry was indeed a departure from the average Pentecostal preacher of his day. He was a trained orator who was highly educated and cultured. This credibility drew many who would usually never attend Full Gospel meetings.

He used intriguing preaching and divine healings to set the stage for massive crowds to accept Christ and be baptized in the Holy Spirit. The healing services were given front-page attention by leading newspapers in the United Stated and Canada.

His messages were in such demand that he began to preach from a second pulpit, this one made of paper. Each of his 20 books ran into multiple editions, with *The Real Faith* being continuously printed for almost 60 years. Discovering the power of the printed page, Dr. Price began a monthly magazine that ran for 40 years.

Dr. Price's writings still possess a contagious faith that enable the reader to climb to new levels of belief in God. The two books included in this volume, *The Meaning of Faith* and *The Sick Are Healed*, have been out of print for over half a century. They are viewed by many to be among the greatest writings ever penned on faith and healing.*

Tim Enloe

* Excerpted from the book *Dr. Charles S. Price: His Extraordinary Life and Ministry*

Part One

The Meaning of Faith

Chapter 1

The Collapse of Faith

ithin the memory of most of us is the time when both the Church and the world seemed to possess certain of the elements of faith. With the dying of the Victorian era the Church seemed to be impregnated with the spirit of evangelism. The great preachers of Christendom thundered forth the truths of God; and in stately cathedral, as well as village chapel, worshipers listened to sermons that were vitalized with faith in God.

Even though they had long since passed away, the preachers who followed the great Reformation continued to live and to exert their influence in the lives of the men who had followed them. They might have differed on questions of church government, and in some instances on doctrinal interpretation, but every one of them could sing lustily, "Faith of Our Fathers," and on the great fundamentals they stood together as one man.

The influence of that Church was felt throughout Christendom. As a matter of fact, the dynamics of its preaching exerted an influence in every country under the sun. In the chronology of God it was undoubtedly the era of Philadelphia. Without question it was the Philadelphian Church. It was the age that contributed more to revivals, to foreign missionary enterprise, to the opening of city missions, to street meetings—and to other channels of aggressive service—than any preceding age since the days of the apostles.

Scintillating like stars in the heavens are the names of illustrious men of faith—firebrands of God's truth who crossed the burning sands of India, surmounted the great wall of China, penetrated the dark jungles of Africa, and raised the standard of the cross in every continent and on every isle of the sea. It was a day of aggressive Christianity. It was the time when the Holy Spirit, with miracles of confirmation, inspired thousands of soldiers of the cross to do wonderful exploits in the name of the Lord Jesus Christ. It was, in short, an era of faith. God called it "Philadelphia."

Then came the deluge. Like the breaking down of the walls of a mammoth dam, the floodwaters of unbelief, of doubt, and of fear surged, and raged, and roared as they flowed irresistibly on, carrying everybody and everything in their cataclysmic flow. Nobody escaped, in world or in church, except those who climbed to the spiritual high places and beheld with consternation, and with broken hearts, the raging, swelling waters that were at their feet.

They saw the things that they had built through the service of the past years collapse like a house of cardboard before the fury of the storm. Ideals, moral standards—the faith of the fathers—were all relentlessly carried away on the shoulders of the tempest to be deposited on the plains of Laodicea, or in the dark valleys of atheism and unbelief.

Previous to that time even the world had some degree of faith. Men who never entered church believed in it. There were some Voltaires and a few Thomas Paynes, but the average man on the street, even though he was unsaved, believed in God and acknowledged the power of salvation. The churches were well attended; the hymns that were sung vibrated with gospel truth; the prayers were fervent; and nearly everybody believed that God was in His Heaven though all was not well with the world. That, of course, was before the deluge.

A great many people blame the World War [World War I—*Editors*] for the collapse of the church, and especially for the collapse of the faith of the average man in the church and in spiritual things. The World War was undoubtedly the climax, but there were many contributing factors that preceded it. There had been a battle for some time against spiritual wickedness in high places.

Thomas Payne, the agnostic, had called it an age of reason. Huxley, with his scientific turn of mind, had attacked the citadels of faith with the broadswords of his intellectual concepts. Darwin had given us his *Origin of Species*, and though he was ridiculed and repudiated by most of the church and many men of science, yet he kept pounding away with his theory until it began to take disastrous effect. The Church for a long time held its ground, although there were some minor surrenders on the battlefield of human life.

The universities entered into the conflict, and so-called professors began at first to insinuate their diabolic and unreasonable teaching, and by innuendo attempted to corrupt the rising generation of that day. Those boys were to become the cannon fodder on the battlefield of the greatest war that the world has ever known. The seed had been planted in the heart and mind, but it had not yet brought forth full fruitage. It is a fundamental law of the eternal God that if there is a sowing there must be a harvest. What a terrible and tragic harvest it was!

The Church had been preaching peace and safety. The philosophers of the world had declared that we were too highly civilized to slay each other upon the battlefield. I have been in the Peace Palace at the Hague; and as I walked along its corridors and beheld the contributions that the nations of the world made to its furnishings, the pictures on the wall seemed to laugh at me; the books held me in scorn (thousands of them were on the subject of international peace); and yet every one of them had stood upon the same shelves while their open ears could listen to the thundering of the artillery and the tramp, tramp, tramp of marching feet. The press and the pulpit had joined hands and both declared that war was an outlaw and would never be tolerated in a civilized world, but that the so-called civilized world was forgetting God.

Reason was rooting up the flowers of faith from the garden of the soul, and planting in their places the brambles and the cacti of doubt and unbelief. Then, I say, came the final conflagration. A world that went to bed under the smiling of the summer sun was awakened by the roaring and raging of the god of war. When the fighting was over—when the millions of corpses had been buried—when the green fields of France had been dyed a crimson hue—when the stately cathedrals of more than one ancient city had been demolished—when the cries of the widows and orphans and homeless had sounded around the world—what was left of the manhood of Christendom came limping home. From that day it was a different world. Bitterness was in the heart and unbelief in the soul. "If there was a God," they reasoned, "how could He allow such things ?"

Underneath the exterior of culture they had beheld the savage instincts of man and they began to declare that Darwin was right. God was not our father—we came from the apes. They had seen the snarl of the gorilla on more than one human face. A world that had become deluged in blood and that had experienced such venomous hate could never have been created as recorded in the Book of Genesis by the will of an eternal and omnipotent God. Having thrown that out they started whirling around in the space of their own misconceptions. So things went from bad to worse!

It was bad enough when the young manhood and young womanhood of the years of the war began to harbor its thoughts and feelings. It was worse when the teachers carried it into the public schools. But it was tragic and blasphemous when it climbed the pulpit steps and started to speak through human lips to congregations who had supposedly come to worship God.

One of the troubles with humanity is that it is oftimes too lazy to do its own thinking. We ride in the automobile somebody else has made for us. Many a young man will tear along the country road at 75 miles an hour, knowing nothing whatever about the principle of internal combustion or the relationship of piston displacement to drive shaft and gear. Many a man will ride in the car of the creed of another's manufacture, without knowing anything about the machine in which he rides.

When the preachers mounted the pulpit steps of what was once a church but had now deteriorated into a social club or an academy of science, the people started assimilating their teaching because they had been used to allowing the preachers to do their thinking for them. This condition, as I have before stated, was not brought about overnight, but it was the result of years of premeditated attack upon the Church by the forces of infidelity and darkness.

The eternal Son of God Himself had looked down the corridors of the years and beheld this very day and hour, and asked the question: "When the Son of Man cometh, shall He find faith on the earth?" The inferential answer, of course, is no. That does not mean, however, that there will be none at all, but it does mean that most of it will be gone. It does declare that what the Church once had it would have lost, to a large extent at any rate.

That statement is proved by the context as contained in Luke 18:1-8. The blessed Master in this Scripture was telling of the widow who importuned the judge over and over again until he avenged her of her adversary. The argument that left the lips of the Man of Galilee was that if an earthly judge would do that, merely because a woman kept coming again and again with her petition to him, would not our heavenly Father avenge that little company who would be true to Him in those days of lack of faith and spiritual declension that would precede the second coming of Jesus?

Thank God, there will be some faith left! Thank God for the great fact that there will be a spiritual ecclesia preceding the second coming of Jesus, just as there was a called-out company immediately following the first physical presence of our dear Lord on the earth.

Thus it was the deluge came. Thus we see reason enthroned in our schools and colleges to the overthrow of faith. Thus it is I feel led by the Spirit to charge the modernistic preacher of our day with high treason to the King of glory and with spiritual assassination of tens of thousands of our people.

Thus it is that the devil laughs at a world that has lost its faith in the Church—and jeers at a Church that has lost its faith in the living God—and beckons them both to his fiery and eternal domain. Thus it is that the Sunday theaters are crowded and the preachers wring their hands and cry, "What shall we do?" as they gaze at their empty pews. Thus it is that the automobile siren has drowned out the pealing of the church bell and the highways are full and the house of God is practically empty.

Thus it is that the angels have hid their faces with their wings as they have beheld the church rolling down the mountainside of time from the peaks of Philadelphia until, bruised and battered and bleeding, it has found itself in the dark, dismal valley of Laodicea.

But there is another side of this story: Thank God for that! There are still some preachers left who believe that Jesus was born of a virgin—and I am one of them. There are still some ministers left who declare that salvation is through the shed blood of Jesus on Calvary's cross—and I am one of that number.

There are still some people left who are willing to be called fools and imbeciles and nitwits, because they believe that Daniel was put into a lion's den and that Jonah was swallowed by a great fish. I am one of that number. There are still some heralds of gospel truth that have beheld the light through the darkest night and are bold enough to proclaim the breaking of millennial day. I belong to that holy company.

That is why I am writing this book. That is why I pray that it will fall into the hands of boys and girls, of high school students, of young men and women, of old men and old women, who are nearing the sunset of their lives—and that it will be a help and an inspiration for them to cling to the faith of their fathers.

Every cloud has a silver lining and there is a garment of light hidden away behind the dark shadows of our day.

James Russell Lowell, in his poem, "The Present Crisis," declares:

> "Ceaseless seems the great avenger,
> History's pages but record,
> One death struggle in the darkness
> Truth forever on the scaffold,
> Wrong forever on the throne—
> Yet that scaffold sways the future,

and, behind the dim unknown,
Standeth God within the shadow,
Keeping watch above his own."[1]

Endnote

1. James Russell Lowell, "The Present Crisis," quoted in *Bartlett's Familiar Quotations*, 16th Edition, Justin Kaplan, Gen. Ed. (Boston: Little, Brown & Company, 1992), 485.

Chapter 2

The Meaning of Faith

*F*or centuries men have been trying to define faith. Dictionaries and encyclopedias have given us their definitions, but in every one of them there is something lacking. That something is the presence of the Holy Spirit, without whose illumative power no man can understand the meaning of faith.

In Hebrews 11:1 the Bible defines it in a two-fold way. It declares that it is "the substance of things hoped for" and "the evidence of things not seen." These were the definitions of a man who had been closeted with God for three years somewhere in the Arabian wilderness, and who for the past 30 years had been led by the Spirit into the deeper revelations of Christian experience and life.

No wonder that the unregenerate man does not understand these Pauline statements. It is not at all strange that the majority of people are unable to drop the plumb line of their thinking to the profound depths of these great truths. The fact of the matter is that faith covers such a tremendous territory and operates in so many ways that it is almost impossible to define it in twentieth-century language. But let us pray that the Holy Spirit will illuminate our hearts and minds and reveal to us by His power those things that could never be apprehended or understood because of our human limitations.

First of all, faith is a persuasion of the mind resting upon evidence. God never asks us to believe anything unless He furnishes a basis for that belief. God never would ask us to believe a lie. So to be sure we do not believe a lie He gives us the truth. He tells us in *what* to place our faith. "Come let us reason together, saith the Lord" is a truth that can be found on every page of the Bible. Faith must have a foundation upon which to rest. In the very nature of things there must be some cause for its operation and some premise upon which it can manifest itself.

A great many people have never understood the difference between presumption and faith. Presumption is belief without evidence and faith is belief in action with it.

Let me illustrate what I mean. Some years ago when I was in a certain Canadian city a scoffer approached me when I was spending a quiet day at the beach. I had been preaching "faith" to thousands of people in a great arena. In spite of the fact that many miracles of healing were wrought by the power of God, there were numbers who were so blinded by the god of this world that they could not see the thing that was happening before their eyes. This man was one of them.

Approaching me as I was reclining on the beach he said, with a sarcastic sneer in his voice, "Oh, you man of faith, why don't you walk out on the water? If you walk out on the water I will believe—I'll stand up tonight before your audience and confess I have been wrong, and I'll give up my job and start preaching."

What would have happened if I had been foolish enough to have taken that man at his word and attempted to have walked on the sea? To have done so would have been presumption. You say that I might have had faith in God and that He would have borne me up. I do not believe it.

There is a great deal of difference between *testing* God and *trusting* Him. I would sink, and what is more, I would *deserve to sink*. There was no promise of God—no scriptural foundation, nothing in Heaven or in earth that would authorize me to attempt so foolhardy a thing.

Yet Peter walked on the sea and the waves held him up. He based his faith on the call of Jesus. In other words, he was persuaded in his mind—

he believed—because the Lord *told him* to do it. The statement of Jesus—the invitation of the Christ—was the foundation upon which Peter's faith was built. The difference between Peter and myself regarding the challenge of the man to my walking on the sea and Peter's actual doing the same, was that he had some foundation for his faith and I had absolutely none.

There is nothing more sure—there is nothing in Heaven or in earth any more reliable than the multitudinous promises contained in the Word of the Lord.

"How firm a foundation,

Ye saints of the Lord,

Is laid for your faith

In His excellent Word!"

What God has said, *He* means. Back of every one of the promises of the Bible is that eternal omnipotence that created every material thing that exists in all the universe. The God who made the things that are out of nothing, and who brought cosmos out of chaos, is the author of His promises and the omnipotence behind every one of them.

The Scripture teaches us that the man who comes to God with his supplications must first believe that He is. That means that he must believe that there is a God—eternal—omnipotent—omnipresent. The man who denies Him cannot possibly have faith in Him. The man who does not believe in Him cannot possibly have the superstructure of faith in his life, for God alone is the author of faith. You cannot rest upon nothing. Only God Himself would have the power of accomplishing that. Jesus, we know, is the author and finisher of our faith. The Bible rings with the clarion call, "Have faith in God—have faith in Christ," thereby signifying that God Himself should be the foundation and the basis for all of our faith. There can be no faith in God without God Himself. Without God Himself faith would be presumption.

Faith always proves itself. It is a leap into the dark, but it lands you in the light. It is a journey into the unseen, but it leads to the heavenly vision. It may be sometimes mysterious in its processes, but it always proves itself in its ultimates. It cannot operate without accomplishment. To continue to exercise faith without some degree of manifestation of its operation means there is something wrong somewhere, and we must find out both how and why.

Chapter 3

The Walls of Jericho

*L*ong and hard had been the years that had elapsed since the Children of Israel halted at Kadesh-Barnea. Forty summers had come and gone and forty winters had they endured since last they were at the portals of the Promised Land. Out on the vast Arabian desert the bones of thousands of them bleached beneath the burning sun, for only the small boys of 40 years ago were men now at the doorway to the land of promise.

They were about to engage in a battle. They had lost one 40 years before. They had fought no army—there had been no attack of infantry; there had been no battalion of soldiers arrayed against them on the hillside—but they had been defeated just the same. Disorganized, whipped, and discouraged, they had turned their backs upon the land that they might have possessed and had lost themselves in the barren vastnesses of the wilderness.

Only two men who were grown at the time of that defeat were now standing before the gates of Jericho. Those two men—Joshua and Caleb—had been warriors of faith. They were here now because God had not forgotten the hoisting of the banner of faith as it fluttered in the breeze of unbelief, waving defiance against all the forces of darkness.

What was the battle that they had lost? It was not fought upon the battlefield of Kadesh-Barnea. It was not waged in the vales of Eshcol. The battle that they lost was fought on the battlefield of their hearts. Reason had overthrown faith, and had defeated the purpose of God. If they had only known it faith would have been the victory. Faith is the victory now, even as it was then.

Faith cried, "Those men are as grasshoppers before us"; but reason shouted, "They are giants and they will overwhelm us." Faith opened its ear to the voice of an eternal Father as He called upon His children to go forward and to trust Him. Reason listened to the growling and sneering of the sons of Anak while the fogs of unbelief hid their vision of God. Faith remembered the pillar of cloud and had not forgotten a pillar of fire that had guarded and guided them on their pilgrim way. But reason had seen the fire in the eyes of the giants of the walled cities and had forgotten the fire that came from the throne of Heaven. Faith had discerned the form of God as He wrapped the cloud around Him for a garment, but reason had looked so long at the walls of the fortified cities; in its mind the cloud was so big it blotted out all vision of Heaven.

So the years had come and gone. I wonder how many times Moses had told them, as they wandered through the wilderness, that faith was the only victory. I wonder on how many different occasions he had declared that only in the strength of a God who could deliver could they ever conquer. Perhaps this generation that had been born during the pilgrimage would believe more than had their fathers in the integrity of the divine word and the omnipotent power that was behind it. The Bible account does not tell us, but if it is true that man is but a composite of his yesterdays, then something must have happened to the new soldiers who found themselves at the doorway of the Promised Land, or was it, perhaps, that man's extremity was at last to prove God's opportunity?

Was it that having exhausted every other resource and having found nothing but blind ends to every trail, they had turned back to the God of their emancipation? Forty years wandering in the wilderness must have incapacitated them as soldiers. Men do not walk over the burning sands without feeling the burning in their feet.

Late one night Joshua, the general, left the camp. Two miles away he could see in the pale moonlight the grim citadel of Jericho, with its walls standing like sentinels, crying, "They shall not pass." His heart must have been filled with anxiety and with bewilderment.

During the past 40 years the problem had not changed one bit. The traveling through the wilderness had not removed the difficulty. If anything, it might have increased it. Of what was he thinking when in the loneliness of that hour he surveyed the distant walls of Jericho? The city was to be taken. There could be no doubt about that. The city must be taken. Of that thing he was certain and sure.

Suddenly, perhaps from beneath the shadows of a nearby palm grove, there appeared by his side a man who had a drawn sword in his hand. Quick as a flash of lightning the challenge fell from Joshua's lips. Marvelous and wonderful indeed is it to know that obedience will bring courage, and walking in the light will banish fear.

Beautiful and yet firm were the words of the enigmatic stranger, "Nay, but as captain of the Lord's host am I come." The heart of Joshua bounded within him. Here indeed was the angel of the covenant. Here was the positive proof that God had not forsaken his people. Faith was the victory that was to storm the walls of Jericho, and unfurl the flag of Israel from the topmost peaks of the citadel.

Then the two had a conference. The captain of the host of the Lord outlined the plans for the taking of the city. The battle was to be the Lord's, and the children of Israel were to walk in the light of faith and leave the results with God. What strange military tactics these two planned together! The like of that plan had never been known in human history, and the method of taking the city was one that every general in the world except Joshua would have laughed to scorn. There was to be no fighting—just walking in obedience.

There could have been no walking in obedience if there had been no God in whom Joshua could have placed his faith. What a test it must have been for Joshua in this particular case. "Faith is the victory," rang the bells in Joshua's heart. "Faith is the victory," sang the choirs of Heaven, and the strains must have floated down to the ears of the lonely man who stood gazing at the distant walls on that moonlit night.

The walls were actually up around old Jericho, but they were down in the spiritual vision of Joshua. Faith was even then the substance of things hoped for. Back he went to camp. "We have won the victory," declared Joshua. "Are the walls down?" answered the soldier. "Have the inhabitants of the city fled?" "No, they are still there, but nevertheless the Lord has delivered the city into our hands."

Chapter 4

How Faith Works

*T*hen he proceeded to unfold the plans of God before a people who should have trusted in the same Lord 40 years before. Spiritual victories are generally won by the operation of the principles of faith that, in the minds of scientific men, are absolutely and thoroughly inadequate.

Reason might have started in again and said, "Listen to me, Joshua, how absolutely ridiculous and unutterably foolish for you to believe that those walls will fall down because you carry a box with you and march around the city. Is it not absurd to believe that blowing trumpets and shouting at the top of your lungs will do anything more than use up all your wind, and can have no effect whatever on those impregnable barriers of stone?"

But faith leaped to the fray in Joshua's heart. He might have replied, "Prate not to me of the reasons of any finite conceptions. The God of all eternity and infinity has spoken. With Him I shall march around the city. I can march and He can push the walls down."

So reason gave way before the affirmations of faith and seven days went swiftly by. Hardly had the shout left the throats of the victorious throng before the angels in Heaven beheld another cloud. It was a cloud of dust rising from the debris of the falling masonry; and Joshua knew that somewhere hidden in that cloud was the arm of the Eternal God, whose name was Jehovah-Nissi.

Have you ever stood before the Jericho of your life? Has the impossible ever loomed up before you with its impregnable walls? Have you ever been face to face with difficulties that in the natural were insurmountable and reason cried, "You might as well capitulate—you might as well give up—there is no use fighting against the inevitable." You might have allowed reason to pass judgment upon you. Have you wandered in the wilderness seeking in vain for the things that you have lost?

There will never be a victory over something else tomorrow until you have first conquered the thing that has defeated you today. God will never let you take a walled city in Arabia after you have been defeated in Canaan. One must go back first to that Canaan issue and settle that question first.

Do not say it cannot be done. Do not be defeated in your soul by the thing that seems to be. *All things are possible to the man who believes.* Belief begets obedience, and obedience builds the road down which faith marches with glorious triumph. Obedience works, but faith is the inspiration that vitalizes it.

So it is we face our Jerichos. In the loneliness of our own souls we stand in fearful contemplation gazing at what seems to be the impossible. In the calm of a moonlit night beneath the shadow of a wall of stone, does the Son of God appear to you? Perhaps as you turn over the pages of His Word in the quiet of your own room there falls upon your burdened soul a benediction like rain upon the thirsty land. Did you get a vision of the captain of the host of the Lord? Is He for you or against you? What a question! He is always, always, always for you. Have you courage ? Have you strength ? Have you faith? He is always and eternally working for your good.

As you feel the pressure of His hand you notice that there is a nail print in it. You listen to the cadency of His voice vibrate with understanding and yet pulsate with power. "Let us plan this thing *together*," He says. "You cannot do this thing alone. You cannot accomplish this purpose by yourself. *We together* will take Jericho." You know it is there—this Jericho of sin—this city of unbelief, this city of seemingly impregnable fortresses, this impediment to your Christian progression and your growth in grace. So it is that you talk with God.

No sooner has the voice of the Savior ceased speaking to the spiritual ear than reason laughs and says, "Isn't it absurd? Isn't it foolish? How can these things be?" But you raise the bugle to your lips and the regiments of joy and of peace and of glory start marching across the fields of your soul. You have not won the victory, and yet you have. The problem is not solved and yet you are shouting because you know it will be. The difficulty has not been removed and yet you are so happy that you can jump for joy. "Faith is the victory," ring the bells in your heart as they did in Joshua's. "Faith wins the victory," sing the choirs of Heaven to you as they sang to Him. The organ peals, "Onward, Christian Soldiers," and the general of faith strides at the head of the marching battalions of the soul.

You might not believe in ministering angels, but I do. You might not believe that they come to the man of faith to dispel all the difficulties of doubt, fear, unbelief, but I do. So it is that you plan it together. You and Jesus—Jesus and you. Your way has become His way. Your plan has become His plan. His voice has inspired you to obedience and you are just as sure that the walls *will fall* on your march on the first day as you are that they have fallen when the sun sinks on the westen hills at the close of the seventh day.

There is not much difference between the shouts of anticipation before they crumble and the shout of victory after they are down. "Faith is the substance of things hoped for, and the evidence of things not seen." So you march together, you and Jesus—Jesus and you—and you walk by His side, even though He is invisible, along what might be the rocky paths of implicit obedience—then one day it happens. The impossible has been accomplished. The difficulty has been overcome. The impediments have been overcome. The impediments have been moved out of the way. The natural has bowed before the supernatural. The finite has acknowledged Him as the Lord.

The walls of your Jericho have fallen and crumbled, not merely because you shouted—not merely because you walked around—an eternal God had something to do with it. In your heart you knew that the cloud of dust that the eyes of the people of the world could see was only a cloak that was wrapped around the omnipotent arm of the Lord. So like Job of old you sat on the front porch of your spiritual possessions richer than you ever were before in all of your life and you said, "This is the victory that overcometh the world, even our faith."

So it was that the walls of Jericho fell then; and by faith today the towering heights that loom up between us and the city not made with hands, crumble to the ground and prove an obstacle against us no more. There are a few steps in the development of the faith that brings the victory that I wish to draw to your attention in the following chapter.

Chapter 5

The Steps of the Ladder

*F*aith must begin by the acknowledgment of our own weakness and inability. In the realms of human attainment, there might be some virtue in the teaching of the philosophers that faith in one's own self and in one's own ability is an asset. In the realm of spiritual life it is a distinct and definite liability.

Man being a finite being cannot reach out of the boundaries of finity and appropriate the things that belong to infinity. The thing that he needs for the development of his soul, however, are not the things that belong to this world. He is absolutely powerless in the grip of sin. To deny the fact of sin or to attempt to repudiate its effect, even though you admit its evidence, is absurd. If a man believes that he can work his way into Heaven, he will never feel his need of a Savior. If he never feels his need of a Savior, how can he have faith in One who came to save him?

Faith begins where sight ends. If you can imagine for one moment that you can take your Jericho without any help from the Lord he will let you try it, but let me assure you you will try in vain. You might walk around it for seven years, or an eternity for that matter, and all you would do would be to strengthen the foundation.

When self-reliance dies, faith begins to be born. When you come to the end of yourself you arrive at the beginning of God in your life. The apostle Paul declared that he could do all things, but he went on to say that he could only do them through Chirst. That is why he was willing to glory in his infirmities—because when he had them the power of Christ rested upon him. For this reason he declared he was the strongest when he was the weakest. This truth is an eternal paradox in the hands of faith.

If your own indomitable will has prevented you from bending the knee then ask God for grace and strength to bring it to obedience. If the devil of pride has been singing its praises in your open ear then banish him forever. Just simply throw up your hands and quit. Come yourself as a miserable, wretched sinner in need of God's power in your life, and ask God to let you see to the end of yourself!

Faith always begins by acknowledging that *you* cannot do it. It is always preceded by a deep feeling that the thing desired is impossible in itself. As Joshua stood that night before the walls of Jericho he might have said in his heart, "I cannot, I cannot do it"—and then the captain of the Lord's host stood by his side and whispered, "No, Joshua, you cannot do it, but *we* can." Such a day in your life will be the birthday of faith. How can you be afraid when your Father is so near?

Then faith must of necessity call upon God. Do not wait for God to call upon you, but you call upon God. The reason that many people never have God in their homes is because they have never invited Him. Before He will confess you you must confess Him. Faith needs God and therefore it calls upon Him.

How foolish we are, poor little creatures of time, to try to get along with our own limitations when there are the immeasurable resources of Heaven at our disposal. Why try to walk the paths of the unchartered future when One is willing to walk by our side who has been every step of the way before?

How my heart bleeds in pity and in sympathy for the young man or the young woman into whose spiritual veins has been injected the venomous poison of unbelief while attending some of our modern educational institutions. Lead your professors to the lawn outside the school and ask them to grow one little tiny blade of grass. Ask them to make a synthetic seed that will sprout and bring forth a harvest. Ask them to make a leaf that will cast away the dress of green it has worn all summer and array itself in the deepest tones of golden brown as it puts on its autumnal clothes. Ask them to fashion one little snowflake or to persuade some hen to hatch her eggs in 14 days instead of 21.

Oh, the corruption of vanity—oh, the absurdity of intellectual pride! The priest who took me through St. Peter's, architecturally the greatest cathedral in the world, swept his arm toward the dome and said, "This is the creation of Michelangelo." But I walked outside, away from the unchallenged magnificence of what I had seen and looked up into the starry heavens. I was on the pavements of Vatican City in faraway Rome. I lost sight of the majesty of St. Peter's and forgot to think about the vaunted temporal power of the Pope as I looked up into the canopy of the skies and said, "This is the creation of my Lord." Yonder blazed hundreds of millions of suns. Stars had been thrown across the immeasurable spaces of the sky like seeds that had been scattered by the hand of the farmer in his field. Worlds were so big and planets were so huge that this little revolving earth fades into insignificance in comparison. Yet that great, vast, immeasurable, multitudinous constellations of stars and planets with moons and suns without number are all moving, moving, moving along the lanes of their appointed and predestined travel.

More than one brain has broken in trying to comprehend it. The next time your pompous professor sticks out his puny chest and tells you that those stars just whirled themselves into position and prates about the anthropoid hypothesis, just lead him outside, ask him to call together the combined intellects of the intelligentsia of the world, and ask them to grow one little blade of grass. Only God can make a tree. Your professor can make a statement—but only God can make a rosebud.

Then faith must get on its knees and cry out to God. Faith must walk down the vales of self-abasement and humiliation in order that it might climb the mountain of divine revelation that is on the other side. Before you can become strong you have to become weak. Before you can be filled you have to be empty. When you have become strong you will rejoice in your weakness. After you have become filled you will thank God for your emptiness. That, I say again, is why Paul rejoiced in his infirmities.

In the third place, faith discovers what God's plan is and *then does it.* How multitudinous have been the plans of men. They sit today in the crumbling castle of their philosophic and scientific theories witnessing what they themselves admit to be the cataclysmic collapse of civilization.

We have had in recent years an epidemic of cultists, of philosophers, of psychologists, of psycho-analysts—until the house they built blew up as they blatantly contradicted one another. In the realm of finance and monetary systems the past years have treated us to the fantastic sight of a succession of experiments that have resulted in nothing at all. At last one of the greatest economists has declared, "Nobody knows anything about money." That was the end of that!

Even in the realm of spiritual things the church officials got to dismantling the machinery of the gospel ship that had carried their fathers and mothers safely to the haven of rest. They started critically analyzing the machinery, and, not being able to understand it, they threw it overboard and began clamoring for a system and method that was amenable to reason, and that could be measured by the calipers of science. So overboard went the virgin birth, and after that they threw away the literal resurrection. They cleaned out salvation through the blood, and one by one the miracles fell with a splash into the modernistic sea. They demoted Jesus from captain to teacher, and some of them even told Paul that they did not want to hear from him anymore, as some of his doctrines were very unsound and unsafe. So the good Lord could do nothing else but leave them to their own foolish destruction while He called the faithful around him and promised them a safe journey into the harbor of rest, where the angels wait to sing their welcome home by the silver strand of Glory.

Yes, there have been many ways—many, many systems—but God's way is the best way, after all. The plan of salvation has never been improved upon. The paths of time are strewn with the wreckage of man's attempted achievements and they ought to be warnings to the young generation of this day to cling to the faith of their fathers.

Let me repeat that faith finds out the Divine plan and then lives and acts and works accordingly. God's way is better than your way unless you make your way His. We have tried the broken cisterns—and lo, their waters have failed. Place your poor torn hand in the nail-pierced hand of a Savior and let Him lead you out of the vales of bewilderments into the light of the sunshine of eternal realities and truth. He loves you enough to do it if you will let Him.

The next step in the development of our appropriating, acting faith is to *get hold of a promise.* I have before stated that in order for faith to be exercised at all it must be established upon some sure foundation. You could not have faith in a bridge to take you across a chasm unless the bridge was there. When you have faith in God—if you will analyze that faith—you will discover that it is based upon something that God has said. The inheritances of the children of the Lord are the wonderful and marvelous promises of the Bible.

Whatever your condition, my friend—whatever your sorrow, whatever your trouble, whatever your heartache—there is a promise in the Word of God to meet it. If you are clothed with the garment of mourning God has promised to give you the robes of praise. If you are traveling through the darkness of the night of misunderstanding, God has promised that He will lead you to the mountain peaks of glory where eternal sunlight gleams. If you are bewildered in the vales of ignorance and misunderstanding and you need wisdom, God has said in His Word that you can come to Him and He will impart it.

If all of the promises were taken out of the Bible—if there was nothing there but a record of the ministry of Jesus and the acts of the apostles—how dismal and dark would be the path our feet would tread. Our religious experience would only consist of the contemplation of the historic Christ. We read that Jesus walked with the disciples. That is history. But when Jesus says, "Lo, I am with you alway, even unto the end of the world," that means experience. Taking hold of that promise, faith says, "Lord, I believe—you are near me—you are by my side"—and thousands of us can testify that that is literally true. When we read that Jesus walked the Emmaus Road and the hearts of the two disciples burned within them as He talked to them by the way, that is history. But your town has an

Emmaus Road, and your hearts have burned within you as He talked with you by the way. That is experience brought by the alchemy of the power of faith.

Some years ago I sat in the home of a young Christian. That is, she was young in Christian experience, but not in years. Only three weeks before she had given her heart to Jesus and had begun to walk the pilgrim pathway that leads to the land of endless day. I have met very few people in my life who were so ignorant of the Bible and of the rudiments of Christianity as was that dear woman. She was indeed a babe in Christ.

She had the misfortune to be the mother of a daughter who was suffering from an incurable disease. The girl had been a great trial and burden to her through life, but with a mother's tender, loving care she had done her best for her ailing child. Only a day before I visited the home her husband had been instantly killed, and her nephew, who was visiting them at the time, severely injured in an automobile accident.

So it was I sat in that home that rainy night. The poor woman sat moaning and wringing her hands and I was doing my best to comfort her. She seemed not to be listening to what I said, but was simply lost in her hopelessness and despair. When I told her of the great Burden Bearer, she mournfully shook her head. I felt led by the Spirit to read from the Word and so I turned to that wonderful Psalm, "He that dwelleth in the secret place." As I read on, emphasizing the words I thought she ought to hear, she suddenly stopped me. A strange look came into her eyes, and she exclaimed, "Does it really say that?"

Turning to the New Testament I read one after another the promises of Jesus. Her eyes opened wider and wider until at last she exclaimed, "To whom did Jesus make that promise?" I reached forward, grasped her hand and looked into her eyes and said, "To you." She leaned back in the chair and repeated over and over again, "That promise—to me; that promise—to me." As the realization dawned upon her faith began to grow as she exclaimed, "Well, if Jesus said He would do that I am—going to ask—him—to—do—it—*for me.*"

Into that home of sorrow came the comforting Nazarene! Into a situation where no earthly circumstance could bring joy by any stretch of the imagination there came a beautiful and an abiding peace. She told me that after the funeral she could not weep except tears of joy. She said, "Is it not strange that joy because my husband found Jesus has exceeded my sorrow in losing him?" I told her it was strange for the people of the world, but it is not strange for the people of God. It is what they ought to expect.

Oh faith, beautiful faith, born of the love of a Father's heart, lift us above the vales of sorrow, and even here wipe the tears from every eye. Glorious faith—wonderful faith—that reaches into the treasury of the divine Word and grips with its fingers some jewel of a promise and presses it against a broken heart until the healing waters flow. Faith—sweet and glorious faith—that takes from our ears the limitations of sound and time—and bids us listen to the music that comes from beside the glassy sea or, perchance, that music that is sweeter still—the voice of our glorified Lord.

Chapter 6

The Key to the Jewel Box

hy walk in spiritual poverty when you have the wealth that is revealed by the promises divine? Why allow a devil to browbeat you and to rob you of your inheritance when you can hold aloft the inspired Word and declare in the face of all the forces of hell, "Thus saith the Lord"?

This promise is mine. You are spiritual millionaires if you only knew it. The promises are yours—the Bible is yours—and Jesus, bless His name, is yours too.

It is not enough to just rock back and forth in your sorrow in the quiet of your own room and have a kind of abstract faith that the Lord *might* help you. God demands activity from His children. "Resist the devil, and he will flee from you," saith the Lord. The reason that he does not flee is because you do not resist him. If you resist him he will go. He may not want to depart, but God will *make him go.*

You see, God *cannot* lie—He must abide by His own word. So it is that faith must emerge from a passive and apathetic state into the realm of activity. Get hold of a promise. Hold it up before God. Tell God it is yours. Tell Him you believe it. Tell Him you are going to hold Him to his Word; *then act your faith.* Walk the next minute and the next day not on how you feel, not influenced by environment, or conquered by circumstances— but walk victoriously with the promises of God beneath your feet. *God has to answer.* God has to do the thing He has promised to do.

In the case of Joshua, as he stood before the walls of Jericho the captain of the host of the Lord had said, "I will deliver Jericho into thy hands." That was all that Joshua needed. If the captain of the host of the Lord had told him to walk on his hands around Jericho he would have done that. Do not believe for one moment that Joshua thought in his heart that the march of the soldiers and the priests would tear down the walls of Jericho. *The march was nothing more than a sign that he believed God.* That is why God had him march. Joshua knew who pushed down those walls, and I know who will push down the walls for you.

But have you given the Lord a sign that you believe Him? Have you begun to act your faith? Have you received the assurance of the falling of the walls, even though God has not yet pushed them over? Anybody can believe that the walls are down, *after* they have fallen. It was within the power of God to have stood by the side of Joshua as he gazed in the distance on that moonlit night and to have said, "Look, Joshua." Then while God pointed His divine finger at the city the walls could have crashed. It would have been just as easy for God to have done it then as for Him to accomplish the same thing seven days later.

Why did he make Joshua wait? The answer is perfectly obvious, but it is of paramount and of tremendous importance. It was because it is part of the economy of God *for man to cooperate with the divine* in the exercising of faith so that God's power might be manifest. If God gave us everything we needed just when we needed it we would deteriorate into spiritual mechanisms. We would become living machines and lose our identity as free moral agents.

Do you not see that it is the man who believes God who gets things from Him? Can you not understand that it is the man who believes God that really honors the Lord by so doing?

George Müller became an apostle of faith because he had the courage to believe God. There can be another George Müller in the days in which we live.

What is your need—what is your problem—what is your question? Unlock the jewel box—unfold the covers of the treasury—there is a promise that is backed by all the eternal resources of Heaven and by all the power of an infinite God. Yes, these things are true, but that promise is backed by something more than that—the Lord God Himself. That is enough for me. Pull that priceless treasure out of its setting and hold it toward the riven skies.

Even though your heart be breaking let your voice ring out, "It is your promise, Lord." Even as you pray, the oil of Heaven will be poured over your wounded heart. There may be, or there may not be, a divine manifestation of the answer—but faith will sing the victory and rejoice in the power of His might. Get that promise—hold it—hold it fast, hold it tight—do not let it go, and march around the walls of your Jericho, with a bugle in one hand and a pitcher in the other. Fill the trumpet with the notes of praise and God will fill the pitcher with the joy of the Holy Ghost. Then you can stand back and watch the Lord push the walls down.

The next step is to remember that in the development of God's economy regarding faith God does not always work in the same way. Let us assume for a moment that He did. Let us assume that God always answers prayer and manifests Himself through His promises in the same amount of time and in exactly the same way on every occasion. Faith would soon die in the human heart, for under such conditions the matter of the fulfillment of the promise would be simply a matter of routine.

God may send the answer before you are through asking today; and tomorrow, for some purpose known to Himself, He may make you wait. But faith on the morrow looks back at the victory of yesterday and says, "Praise the Lord!" It does not agonize as it contemplates the future, but it rests with a sublime peace while waiting for the fulfillment of the divine Word.

If it worried it would not be faith. If it started to become overly anxious faith would strangle itself and soon die in the human breast. Faith can be active when it is at rest—and it can be the strongest when it wears a crown of peace. When the agonizing prayer of intercession turns to the psalm of praise, it is faith that sits at the keyboard and brings melodies from the organ of the heart.

Not very long ago I stood by the ruins of ancient Jericho. Workmen had been busy removing the rubbish and the debris and they had succeeded in uncovering some of the old houses that had been buried during the centuries that have marched by. Just across the road from where I was standing was the spring of water that is known to this day as the Fountain of Elisha. It is recorded in Second Kings 2 that a man of the city of Jericho told Elisha, a man of God, that the water was no good and the ground was barren. The prophet, undoubtedly inspired by the Spirit, instructed them to bring him a new cruse and to put salt in the vessel. When he had done so, Elisha took the vessel of salt from their hands and, walking to the water, emptied the contents of that vessel into it and exclaimed, "Thus said the Lord, I have healed these waters. There shall not be from thence any more death or barren land."

Nearly three thousand years have passed since the day when Elisha obeyed the word of the Lord, but *those waters are still sweet.* That spring pours out a great volume of clear, cool, sparkling water without a single trace of alkali in it. Every other spring in that vicinity is unfit to drink and the alkali with which they are filled stains the nearby ground a chalky white. But this spring—Elisha's spring—pours out a beautiful and steady stream of sparkling water. It irrigates the countryside, and every orange and lemon tree that is irrigated by its flow speaks to me of the promise of God. When our God says "forever," He means just that. He is the same God who has promised you.

So it was I gazed at the ruins of Jericho as I stood just across the road from the bubbling water of a beautiful spring. Somebody turned to me and said, "I wonder if those are the very stones that fell down when Joshua marched around the city?" In reply I exclaimed, "I do not know whether they are or not; but one thing I do know—we can still cry as they cried then, Jehovah-Nissi—the Lord our banner. It is just as true today as it was then. Our little party walked across the road and we drank of the waters of Elisha's fountain. With the moisture still on my lips I turned to my friends and said, "God does not forget." From 895 B.C. to 1936 A.D. is a long time—but the waters are still sweet.

Dear children of God, is not therein a lesson that will strengthen your faith? "Thus saith the Lord" is just as true in 1936 A.D. as it was in 895 B.C. The only difference is that in those days they poured salt, but in these days He pours grace.

Chapter 7

What Is Faith?

We now come to a very important part of our study. We pray for the Spirit to enlighten us, as we carefully and prayerfully answer the question, "What is faith?" What does it mean?

I stated earlier in this book that the best definition of faith is to be found in the Book that tells us all we know about it. It is to be found on the pages of that volume that records the marvelous exploits of faith operating in the hearts of godly men in days gone by. Hebrews 11:1 declares, "Now faith is the substance of things hoped for, the evidence of things not seen." In the Revised Version we read, "Faith is the assurance of things hoped for, [the proving] of things not seen."

In every one of these different translations that, of course, mean fundamentally the same thing, there is a direct statement that faith is established upon and founded upon evidence. Even though the things are not seen they must be there, for if they were not there the Bible would not call them "things." It puts a certain tangibility upon the effect of the operation of faith. Were there to be no evidence there could not be the exercise of faith, but before faith can operate it must of necessity have some hope—some purpose—that requires its operation.

Faith is the assent or persuasion of the mind to the truth of God's revealed will. Faith is the persuasion of the heart to the integrity of the divine Word. Faith is a combination of the belief of the heart and the reasoning of the spiritual mind based upon divine assertions and promises that we believe to be immutable, omnipotent, and infallible. Faith is not naturally reasonable, because being of divine origin it reaches beyond the boundaries of reason into the realms of the supernatural. It is not foolish, except to the man who has no spiritual light, because it is energized and vitalized by the Spirit of God, who will take us beyond the realms of the natural into contact with the supernatural powers that belong to God Himself. For this cause what is unreasonable to the natural man becomes reasonable to the man who is filled with the Spirit.

If all things were self-evident, what need would there be for the exercising of faith? If faith did not take us beyond the boundaries of the things that could be understood by the mind of man without God, there would be no need for us to desire to posses it in the sense that the Bible teaches it. For then, the results could be obtained by the operation of mental faculties alone. That is, if faith never operated in the realm of the supernatural there would be no need for us to have faith in God, because we could get everything we wanted without Him.

But faith not only operates within the boundaries of the things we understand and what our minds can apprehend—but faith operates in the realm of the supernatural. It does the impossible. It reaches far beyond the limits of human attainment and operates outside the scope of mental ingenuity. That is why fools are sometimes wiser than men of education.

The reason that the apostle of old said he was willing to become a fool for Christ's sake was because faith, in his life, was operating in a realm that all the doctors of learning knew absolutely nothing about. They might know the age of the rocks—but he knew the Rock of Ages. They might attempt to look at the stars through a telescope, but the child of God by faith was in constant communion with the God who used them as a throne. Some men by years of study will reach out to a limited intellectual distance, while the child of God will give one jump in faith and land somewhere over on the other side of the wall. It brings the jewels of Heaven and gives them to the creatures of time.

Two men can look at a rainbow. One of them can give you a scientific thesis on the operation of the spectrum on the rain drops that have their prismatic values—while the child of God looks at the same rainbow and sees in it nothing but the promises of God blended in gorgeous colors wrapped around the shoulders of the storm.

Faith is a ladder up which we climb out of the world of things that seem to be into the realms of things as they really are. The transition might not be instantaneous, but the very fact that you climb the ladder proves that you have faith in the ladder to bear you and in the fact that there is something at the top. The top is the thing that is hoped for—every rung of the ladder is a promise of God—but it is *faith* that inspires *to do the climbing.*

The top of the ladder might be beyond the vision of the brainiest and the most keen-sighted man. It has to be—for if they could see it there would not be the need to exercise faith to believe it was there.

My Greek Testament declares that faith is "a conviction of things not seen." What do we mean by this word *conviction?* In the larger and broader sense we mean a persuasion of the heart and mind—for both of them cooperate in the operation of faith. If the things that are not seen are at the top of the ladder and two men are sitting together on the ground at its foot, the man who starts to climb the ladder is persuaded that the thing he wants is at the top. The man who makes no attempt to climb does so because he refuses to believe what he cannot see. If you could see it and climb for it, it would not be faith. When you do not see it, and yet climb for it—that is faith. So faith is the conviction—the persuasion of heart and mind of things *not seen.*

But let me bring you again to our original statement that it *must be based upon evidence.* If a poor old tramp told you that there was a pot of gold at the end of the rainbow you would not believe it—because there would be no evidence. If a millionaire told you on his word of honor that there was a purse of gold awaiting you at his office you would immediately go after it. The act of going after it would be faith in operation following a persuasion of the mind that what he said was true.

Now then, when God says something—God, the eternal one; the Lord of Creation; the one who held the oceans in the hollow of His hand; the One whose fingers fashioned the mountains and traced the course of the rivers down their sides; when God says something and backs it by His authority—then, I submit, *you have a basis for your faith.*

When that eternal One, clothed in glory and majesty and power— before whom devils tremble and flee—before whose majestic words of command even nature suspends its operation—when that God speaks, then I maintain you have a basis, an evidence for the operation of your faith.

When that wonderful Jesus—the Christ of Calvary who was clothed and filled with all the fullness of the Godhead and who bade the angry waves of Galilee be still—when that Jesus speaks and gives you a promise, then I maintain that you have a basis for your faith.

He promises the unattainable and we receive it. He promises the impossible and we get it. An unbelieving world may scoff, modernists may laugh me to scorn—the poor blinded eyes of the super-intelligentsia of this day and hour might not see the working of the Divine—but just the same, I maintain that faith can still remove mountains and that *all things are possible* to the man who believes.

> "Faith, mighty faith, the promise sees,
> And looks to God alone;
> Laughs at impossibilities
> And cries *it shall be done!*"

There are two words in the original Old Testament language that are translated into "trust" and "faith." One of them that is translated "believe," "trust," and "faith," means in the transitive, "to prop up," "to stay," "to support." In the intransitive it means "to stay oneself." The second word that is translated "trust" means "to throw yourself upon," "to cast oneself upon." Both of these meanings have their place in the development of the experience of faith. All faith is built upon one foundation and is fundamentally the same regarding its origin and system of operation.

With regard to these two translations the difference of meaning is very apparent although the operation of faith is just the same. When we say we believe God, we mean that we stay ourselves upon His Word. We believe what He says—in other words, we believe God. Again, when we say we believe *in God* it means that we cast ourselves upon God Himself.

In relationship to faith throughout the whole of the Word these two translations predominate, but remember that God is the objective of both types. In one case it is God Himself and in the other case it is His Word. But the Word without God would not be the Word. It would be robbed of its authority, so we are necessarily led to the ultimate of all the operative faith—God Himself. Is it faith for the lifting of a burden? Who lifts it? God. To have faith in the burden to lift itself would bring no result, but to have faith in the God who can lift it and then to put faith in operation because He has promised to do it is another thing altogether. Can you not see why Jesus is called the author and the finisher of our faith? In other words He is the Alpha and the Omega of our faith. It begins with His promise and ends with the manifestation of His power.

How can a man have faith who believes not in the promise, and how could faith operate if there was not that mighty One who made the promise? That is why it is absolutely impossible for the man who is not walking close to God to exercise faith. The closer you walk, the more abundant faith. The man who travels down the highway of intellectual accomplishments knows nothing but himself and chooses naught but the fragmentary illusions of time. The man who walks in the Spirit contacts the realm of eternal power, for he communes with God Himself. Turn the pages of history over—read your Bibles and biographies of men of faith—and you will find in every instance that they have been men who have walked with God.

In the eleventh chapter of the Gospel of Mark and the twenty-second verse we have the statement of Jesus made to his disciples, "Have faith in God." The marginal reading gives you the translation, "Have the faith of God"—that is the faith that God imparts. This statement very clearly signifies that faith is inseparable from God, and that He alone, through the ministry of the Son and the Holy Spirit, can impart it. The Scripture declares that it is a fruit of the Spirit and the gift of God. It logically and reasonably follows that faith being in God must of a natural consequence be of God.

But it was to man that Jesus was speaking. Did He ever ask him to do the impossible? Did He ever hold out to him an ideal that was unattainable? The answer is amost emphatic no. The modernist will respond with an aggressive yes and declare that the age of miracles is past, and that the day of the alchemy of faith's workings will break no more.

We see, then, that in order to have the faith *of* God, we are taught that we must exercise faith *in* God for the things that are promised us *by* God. We must contact God Himself. That brings us then to another important step in our study, namely: "How to get faith."

Chapter 8

How to Get It

*O*h, how much we need Him! Oh, how our hearts should cry out as we wander through the darkness of our unbelief, until lost in the dark glades of our fears we grasp at vain, imaginary things in our endeavor to get the light.

We have proved that faith is—that God is back of it—that God has an immeasurable supply of it—and it ought to be the purpose of every one of our hearts to possess it. We turn from reading in the Word the account of what faith as big as a grain of mustard seed will do, but we can search the world over and not find as much faith as that outside God Himself. He has it—we know that—but our problem is how to get it. I want to begin this chapter with the emphatic declaration that faith can do anything that God can do. "*All things* are possible to him that believes." There is no limitation to that promise. There are no boundaries to it...it is as deep as the deepest depth and as high as the limitless canopy of space.

In the first place, let me remind you that faith is a gift. That means that it cannot be earned. That means that it does not come merely as a reward for service or as the result of your own struggle and endeavor. We hear a great deal about appropriating faith. Faith can appropriate, but you cannot appropriate faith. Let me remind you once again—the Bible declares *it is a gift.* But you tell me it is also a fruit, and if it is a fruit, then you say that you can grow it. Not so, my friend. It is not a fruit of your growing. It is a fruit *of the Holy Spirit.* You cannot grow the fruit of the Spirit without the Spirit. If you could, then it would not be the fruit of the Holy Spirit but the fruit of your own endeavor—the fruit of your growing. Try as man will, he cannot separate the possession of faith from the possession of God Himself.

In Romans 12:3 the apostle Paul deals very clearly and forcibly with a man who is carried away with spiritual exaltation because of his accomplishments, for he says, "For I say, through the grace given unto me, to every man that is among you, not to think of himself more highly than he ought to think; but to think soberly, according as *God hath dealt to every man the measure of faith.*" Then, again, Paul declares in the First Corinthians 2:5, "That your faith should not stand in the wisdom of men, but in the power of God." In other words, he was declaring that no matter what miracle was wrought—no matter what supernatural manifestation of power was accomplished—he answered as soon as possible because he did not want the people to believe for one moment that it was his work, but he wanted them to know that it was the work of God.

The steps are very clear:

- Faith can move mountains—work miracles—and bring to pass all of those results that are seen through the promises of the Word.

- It is only God Himself who can do this.

- If only God can do it, then, of course, we need God.

- Only to the man who walks with God will He impart and give the faith to bring these things to pass.

Beloved, therein lies the secret of the attainment of faith. Get close to God. Get very close to God. Withdraw yourself from the noise and hubbub and clamor of a world of unbelief and sin—*get alone with God.* Close your ears to the whispers of evil men and plead the blood of Jesus as a barrier against the suggestions of the devil—get alone with God. Pray for the blood to cleanse from sin, and for the heart to be made clean and pure—get alone with God.

The Scripture tells us that the Word of the Lord is a power that sanctifies. With all my heart I cry unto you, "Faith cometh—faith cometh," but how does it come? "Faith cometh by hearing, and hearing by the Word of God."

How wonderful the contemplation of this truth! How glorious and marvelous this assertion of the divine heart! Are you in the dark? His Word is a light unto your feet and a lamp unto your pathway. Are you sick and suffering? He sent forth His Word and healed them. Are you hungry and crying out for that which satisfies? Men do not live by bread alone, but by every word that proceeds out of the mouth of God. Are you lost, groping in the darkness and slipping down the steeps of time toward eternity's night? He alone has the Word of eternal life.

The Word was made flesh and dwelt among us. The miracle of the incarnation got hold of God's love, His heart throb, His compassion, His tenderness and forgiveness. Wrapping it in a little bundle of humanity, He pressed it in a woman's arms in a manger in Bethlehem. The angels of Heaven started to sing because the Word was made flesh. "Faith cometh by hearing, and hearing by the Word of God."

Once again I repeat—get alone with God if you would have faith.

Again let me remind you that if miracle-working, irresistible faith was to be possessed separate and apart from the presence and person of God, man might use it for evil and not for good. God withholds it from the man who desires to use it for his own glory and aggrandizement, but imparts it to the man who wants to use it for the glory and the honor of the name of the Lord.

There have been many cases, as we travel down the corridors of history, of men who have lost their faith because they have lost their God. It is a well known fact that the depth and sincerity of a man's belief is measured by his nearness to God. It is not so much what you know, but what you *are*. God has seen to it that the highways of Glory are open to the illiterate and the poor. It is not contact with intellectual understanding that will bring faith, but it is that beautiful and intimate walk with the One who still will travel with you as he walked with Adam in the garden before sin separated them in the days of the long ago.

More than once in my humble ministry I have done my best to help people through to a possession of the fullness of one of the promises of God. We prayed but the answer did not come. Then, perhaps days later, they have come to me again with a new step—a new light shining out of their eyes—a new resonant ring in their prayer that has ascended to the Throne. Then the bells of praise started to chime; the thing that was hoped for took substance; and the thing that was not seen became a conviction. Happiness and joy broke over the shores of the soul like waves breaking on the sands of the sea. What a difference! What had brought about the change? *They had been closeted with God.* They had discovered that in order to have the faith of God—as Jesus Himself instructed his disciples to do—they must have God Himself.

Get alone with God. He will not disappoint you. Get alone with God. He will not let you down. As you feel the sacred nearness of His presence, and as you listen to the tenderness and understanding tones of His voice, doubts and fears and unbelief will slink away and in their places He will impart the faith that you need.

Not from your agony, not from your groanings, not from your struggles—but from the heart throbs of a Father's heart you will get your faith. You will get it not only because you need it, but because you believe Him. He will impart it. Get alone with God.

Chapter 9

How Faith Grows

*I*t must not be forgotten that while the quality of faith might not be changed, it is certainly possible in the economy of God to increase the quantity.

The reason that the quality of faith cannot be changed is because it is one thing that allows no alloy. Faith mixed with doubt ceases to be faith, and when impregnated by fear very soon loses its potency.

There may be a great many doubts and fears in the human life, but when a man cries out to God in the midst of them, there is faith—some faith, at any rate—endeavoring to reach through. You cannot mingle and merge faith and doubt any more than you can dissolve oil and water. They refuse to cling to each other; one of them will predominate; one or the other is certain to gain the mastery.

The little faith you have today will become the greater faith that will dispel doubt tomorrow if you use it, and refuse to be separated from it. Faith has to be the stronger because God is the author of faith, and the devil and yourself are the authors of doubt and fear. We know that God is stronger than the frailties of humanity and that He is more powerful than all the forces of hell and the devil!

The only way in which faith can grow is to develop it by use. This is a fundamental law in God's economy for the development and growth of spiritual life.

Take for instance, walking in the light. A man cannot walk in the light unless he has contacted the revealed will of God. It might come to him through the voice of the Spirit—understanding through hearing some Holy Ghost sermon—or the unfolding of the riches of the divine Word. To walk in obedience according to the revealed will of God is what we mean when we say that we are walking in the light.

It is generally acknowledged that some men have more light than others. The reason that they have become the recipients of more light is because they have learned the lesson of walking in all the light of the present, so that more light might be given them in the future. If a man refuses to walk in the light today he will discover that tomorrow will be growing dark. If a man will walk in all the light he has today, he will find he will have more light in which to walk tomorrow.

Man must always cooperate with God in the development of his Christian character and in the enrichment of his experience. Light is light in essence and in quality, whether it is great or small. The quantity of faith and the power of it can be increased with each succeeding day.

So it is with faith. To be possessed with an ever-increasing faith one *must make constant use of the faith that they have.* It is not enough to sit idly by—rocking in a rocking chair, or even supplicating on one's knees for more faith. To use the faith you have will honor the Lord Himself and necessitate your keeping very close to God.

It is far better to cry out when doubts and fears are battling what little faith you have, "Lord, I believe, but help Thou mine unbelief." You remember the man in the Bible who said that. There was faith there—not very much, it is true—but still it was there. There was also unbelief there. Unbelief that the man despised, hated, and did not want—but it was still there.

He might have quit and wrung his hands in abject misery and said, "It is no use." Had he done so he would have been defeated. There never would have come to him the victory that must have made him shout for joy when he beheld the power of the Lord. Instead, while acknowledging a load of unbelief he exclaimed, "Faith, get to work. Little faith, get hold of God. Little faith, hear His voice. Reach out and touch Him. Do not let Him go."

Little faith becomes great faith when he commences to use his muscles. Never forget that faith is imparted for a purpose, and refusal to use it for the purpose for which it is given will mean that it will be withdrawn. The man who has lost faith has lost it because he refused to use it.

Like a coward he may blame it upon environment, or upon circumstances. Sometimes I have known men to blame it upon heredity. But Christ is greater than environment—more than a match for every circumstance. Even the chains of heredity are broken by the God of the Lion of the tribe of Judah.

The man who cries around that he has lost his faith has nobody but himself to blame. Remember that God never expects the impossible from any man, and never demands more than a man's capabilities will allow him to render. He will not suffer us to be tempted, or as the Greek says "tested more than we are able to bear." There might not be 50 avenues of escape, but the promise of the Lord is that there will *always be one.*

To the dear people, who through lack of understanding have been sitting around for years waiting for "sufficient faith," I would say without hesitation, "Use the faith you have." It might not be very big, but remember that a little David killed a big Goliath. A little stone of faith from the brook of God's flowing grace can do more than a broadsword of the finest steel forged on the anvils of hell. A little boy carrying a dinner pail with some faith in his heart can accomplish more for God than a whole army who pattern their armor after the fashion of Saul.

How do you know that your faith is not sufficient? Have you tried to find out? What if it does not bring you the answer in as quick a time as your prayer ascended to God? Has it ever occurred to you that if God always answered as quickly as you asked, that your faith would have so little exercise it would never have a chance to grow? You may feel a little pained at the delay, but perhaps they will be growing pains. Keep on keeping on, and you will feel better by and by.

The Word of the Lord is the pasture in which faith can feed and grow. Faith comes *through* the Word and it grows and increases by feeding *upon* the Word. The effect of many a good sermon has been lost and has not acted as an inspiration to faith because people have refused to eat the food of the Word. That assimilated word might have produced faith.

We get too busy with the affairs of the world. Home life and numerous problems manifest themselves and we find very little time for the study of the Word of the Lord. I told you in a preceding chapter that faith cometh by hearing and hearing by the Word of the Lord. To spend a lot of time on our knees praying for faith will not do us much good unless we also go to the place of nourishment—the Word of God. A man would be foolish to pray for physical strength if he did not give some attention to his diet, but insisted on living on nothing but ice cream and pastry.

Reading the Word also brings you in direct and vital contact with the promises of God. The heart becomes persuaded that the promises are true. The Holy Spirit commences to impart faith and the manifestation and exercise of faith makes the promise real.

Reading the Word of God necessarily means that we keep our eyes *constantly* upon Jesus. How many Christians make the mistake of living on the experiences of yesterday. Even a minute can make a difference; Peter found that out while walking on the sea.

The grace of yesterday will not suffice for the problems of today. The power by which we overcame in the days gone by is not the power that is used in obtaining the victory of tomorrow. The stream of water flows fast—your faith is gone. The water that rippled over the pebbles at the bottom of your yesterday is today lost in the vastness of the sea. God's grace is not a stagnant lake. It is a flowing river. The man that David declared was God's blessed man was the man who was like a tree planted by the rivers of water who would give forth fruit in his season.

It is a very common but pernicious habit to excuse our lack of victory today by the testimony of the triumphs of yesterday. There should be an *increase* of faith, an *increase* of spiritual power, a deepening of the experience, and a multiplying or an enrichment of Christian virtues in the human life.

I know the storm clouds lower; I know the problems arise; I know that circumstances harass; I know that the environment is sometimes conducive to fear—but lift up your head, O child of God. Wait not for an army of soldiers of faith to march across the fields of your life; *use what faith you have.* Shout the victory even though the noise of the storm seems to drown your voice and throw it back in your face. The Christ that heard the cries of the man on the Jericho road above the din and noise of the throng has not lost His power to hear. He hears that cry.

You will stand some day in wonderment at the impregnability of the divine Word and the immutability of the eternal promises of God. God cannot lie—God will not withdraw His oath—God will vindicate His Word; and no power on earth or in hell can prevent Him from obeying and fulfilling His own promises.

The best way to increase your faith is to use what faith you have.

Chapter 10

Faith in Divine Healing

*W*e now come to a subject of vital interest: namely, the question of divine healing.

Nobody knows more than I do the tremendous protest that the ministry of divine healing has brought about in the Church of the day in which we live. When some years ago a great revival wave of the ministry of divine healing encircled the entire globe, it was not long until the opposition began to be organized, and every honest and dishonest means was used to try to persuade people against it. Books were written by the score; sarcastic articles filled the columns of the newspapers; and even religious magazines devoted page after page to tirades against the ministry of divine healing. I believe the devil was mad. I believe that he was so angry that he commenced to use every weapon at his command to stamp out the belief in the supernatural power of God relative to the healing of the body.

The revival of divine healing ministry came at the close of the Philadelphian age of the church. It was nothing but a natural result of the glory and power of the Philadelphian era of evangelism and holiness. Practically every one of the great denominational leaders who were stalwarts of the faith were hearty believers in divine healing, and many of them claimed to have been delivered from physical infirmities by the power of God. John Wesley filled his journal with it. Andrew Murray wrote a book about it. John Knox practiced it and preached it as he went like a firebrand through Scotland. Peter Cartwright proclaimed it. In later years men of the intellectual caliber and spiritual power of A.T. Pierson championed this gospel truth.

There was not the slightest doubt about it—people were healed by the power of God. It was proving to be one of the greatest forces for the salvation of souls and for the spreading of the fires of evangelism that the Church had seen for centuries.

No wonder the devil was mad. People could behold with their eyes the mighty works of God. Altars were filled with men and women seeking Jesus Christ as a personal Savior. They were not all after loaves and fishes by any means. When a man testified that he had been changed in soul and in heart, they had nothing to go on except his word of testimony until perhaps his life began to prove his testimony; but when the lame man commenced to leap and the lips of the dumb were loosed—even sinful men opened their eyes in wonderment, and the world began to know that there was a God in Israel. As it was in the days of the apostles that people came running together because they heard of the healings that had taken place, so it began to happen in the days in which we live.

The ultimate aim of a public divine healing ministry was not only to get men healed in body, but to get them to God for the salvation of their souls. The salvation of the soul is of infinitely more importance than the healing of the body. What shall it profit a man if he gain a well body and lose his own soul? Beginning on the day after Pentecost, the disciples, filled with the Holy Ghost and full of faith and of the power of God, began to pray for the sick. They used divine healing as a means of drawing the people and then preaching to them the gospel of a God of marvelous love. No wonder that the fires of revival swept across continents, leaped over the seas, and invaded the isles everywhere.

There is no doubt in my mind but that this was God's plan. He used it then, and if it was legitimate then it certainly would meet with the divine approval now. But years ago John beheld in the spirit the tragedy that was to take place during the closing days of time. While he was sitting on the lonely Isle of Patmos listening to the surging of the sad sea waves, God gave him that glorious and wonderful revelation that supersedes any spiritual revelation of its kind ever given to man. John beheld a radiant church, glorious and wonderful to behold, standing on the mountain peaks of a Philadelphian experience, begin to succumb to the bombardments of the enemy.

It was not the devil of lust that led his force against the citadels. It was not the devil of drink or of vice that stormed the Philadelphian heights. The soldiery of hell wore no armor but instead they clothed themselves with the equipment of the preacher and dipped their tongues in honey as they spoke. The devil sent his emissaries of reason and wisdom and they declared, "Hail, Philadelphia, we have come to thee in the name of the Lord. We are the revealers of truth that you have never discovered. We are the heralds of knowledge such as you have never known. We are friends of God and we wish to unfold to you the deeper understanding—the rational interpretation of the Word that you have never comprehended before."

Philadelphia began to capitulate. It soon closed its prayer meeting to listen to the lectures on science. Then somebody asked for faith, but faith had gone. The light was slowly flickering out and it was easy for it to be enticed along the road of new research until at last it found itself in the vales of Laodicea. It kept up the old forms. It sang hymns—it prayed prayers such as they were—it built the same kind of buildings; but something was gone. Or rather it was *Somebody*. It was the power and the presence of the Holy Ghost. So evangelism left the pulpit and reason climbed the rostrum steps. So faith was banished from the councils and intellectualism started to preach. There was no salvation through the blood, no bodily ascension of the Lord, no personal appearing of Jesus in the clouds of glory—these things were all gone. As for divine healing, if ever there was any, it was for a bygone age.

If anybody testified to the fact that they were healed, the Pharisees of the closing days said, "He casteth out devils by beelzebub, the prince of the devils."

Mothers have come to me with tears streaming down their cheeks, weeping because of the growing unbelief of their sons and daughters. Young men and young women in their teens have sat by my desk and laughed in my face as I have told them that I still believe in the verbal inspiration of the good old Book and all the accounts that are contained therein of the supernatural power of God. They laugh at Mother and call her old-fashioned, and they ridicule Father and declare that he is an old fogy in his religious beliefs, even though he might be a pretty good dad. The modernistic preacher backs them up and declares that we must have a gospel that will fit in with the college needs of this particular day.

What a tragedy! The angels of Heaven must hide their faces as they contemplate such an awful sight. As for myself, I would rather have never known the way—never to have mounted a pulpit step—than to be in the shoes of one of those intellectual giants who have contributed to the spiritual delinquency of the youth of our day. They preach loudly and long about the wrecking of the body while they destroy faith in God and proceed to wreck the soul.

My dear young friend, if such you are into whose hands this book shall fall, let me give you one word of irrefutable logic. The proof of the pudding is in the eating. The proof of the gospel is in what it does. The proof of the Bible is in the fact of the fulfillment of its promises. There might be some basis for your doubt if you prayed to a God who never answered. If there was never a reply, no matter how intently you prayed, then you might have some basis for your assumption that there is no God. When you pray and He answers, you know there *must be* a God. When you pray for healing and healing comes, then you know there must be a Healer somewhere.

With all of my heart I assure you that if you will be honest enough and sincere enough to come, even in your doubt and in your fear, God Himself will recognize the little flickering flame of integrity and sincerity that I know must lie within your breast.

Let me give you this challenge. By following out what the Bible tells you to do, you will experience just what the Bible says you will experience.

God is His own interpreter and He will make plain those spiritual truths that you never have hitherto grasped.

So it is in the realm of divine healing. While others defame and scatter the seeds of doubt and fear—God is still healing people. There are tens of thousands of them who are living today who can testify to the miraculous and supernatural healing power of Jehovah-Rapha. Many of these cases are so evident that even the bitterest enemies of Divine Healing have had to admit that the people have been healed. Oh, how real and wonderful Jesus is to the man who has felt His healing touch! But they deny that a loving healing Savior did it.

Chapter 11

Faith for Healing

*T*he humanity of Jesus overwhelms me—His understanding of our human nature, His great tender heart, His infinite and beautiful compassion. He never would break the bruised reed and no account in Scripture tells us that He ever quenched the smoking flax. The broken heart He never despised, and the faintest cry always found lodgment in His sympathetic ear.

Did ever a man speak as this man spoke? Did ever a heart love as this heart loved? He, who was God, wrapped around His deity the garments of humanity and placed a human hand upon many a fevered brow. Wonderful Jesus—very image of the Father—who came to make the healing waters flow where every thirsty heart could drink. Wonderful, wonderful Jesus!

The records are simply filled with the story of His healing ministry. The Bible is very clear about them—they were miracles of healing for the physical body. In the second place, He distinctly told His disciples that they were to continue in the ministry of healing that He was imparting to them. In clear and plain language they were told that they were to lay hands on the sick and that they should recover. As a matter of fact, it was to be one of the signs that were to follow them that believe. The Scripture is so clear and so plain that a child can understand it. It receives all the authority it needs for the words were spoken by Jesus Christ Himself.

In the next place, after the death, resurrection, and ascension of Jesus, the disciples did exactly what the Lord told them to do. They prayed for the sick and the sick were healed. The Book of Acts is filled with accounts of the miracle-working power of God in relation to the restoration of health to the bodies of men who were sick. In the various epistles divine healing is very clearly taught, and the first president of the first ministerial union that ever convened, the apostle James, wrote plainly and forcefully regarding the position of the Church in this respect. James 5:14 still stands as a lighthouse upon a hill, shining out its welcome beams of truth to every child of God who is suffering from bodily ailment and pain. The lightnings have flashed, the thunders have rolled, the storms of unbelief have reached around the foot of the rock; but the light still shines. There was James 5:14 at the end of the apostolic era and there is still James 5:14 in the day in which we live. Devils in hell, unbelieving men, and faithless preachers have all failed to put out that light.

The Pauline Epistles bring further and added corroboration to those great truths. The ministry of the apostle himself was simply filled with manifestations of the power of Christ to heal.

I understand from the Word itself that no man could ever add to or take away from the words of the completed Book. It is the direct teaching of the Lord that even the Spirit Himself would never again fall on man in such a way as to cause him to add to the inspired Word. God's revealed will as far as the Bible is concerned has been completed and is final. No man has ever been authorized by the Spirit or by virtue of his own understandings to take away from the completed and inspired Word of God.

I would like to ask the critics of divine healing for the chapter and verse in which it is declared that divine healing would ever be taken away from the Church, or that the hour would ever arrive when it would be against God's will for us to pray for the sick. I challenge them to give me one scintilla of scriptural evidence that would lead any man to believe that the commands of the Lord would ever be abrogated and the teachings of the apostle nullified in this respect. They cannot do it, and they know they cannot do it. So they rise up and say—half of a verse is for yesterday and half of a verse is for today. They tell you to take this and throw out that. Who gave them the authority to wield the scissors of criticism on the inspired page? From what source did they get their authority to take from the Word of God?

Here is where faith comes in. Faith—glorious faith—God-imparted faith—looks up oftimes through scalding tears and, holding the Word of the Lord high in its hand toward Heaven, says, "Lord, I believe." When the part can contain the whole, then the mind of man can understand the Bible without the help of the Holy Spirit. When time is longer than eternity, then reason should dethrone faith and establish itself as the emperor of our lives. These things can never be.

There is only one possible way of clearing out the debris and the rubbish of unbelief and of modernistic interpretation from the rooms of our hearts, and that is by the exercise of faith in God. Without the slightest hesitation I declare that the man who wants faith *can have* it. If we are sinners we need not cry in vain. God Himself will fulfill the promises because He perfected the plan. The man who wants to know, by the grace of God *can know*. Light can shine in the darkest place and understanding can come to the heart that has been clouded by the fogs of unbelief.

We are not swayed by any self-desire—we are not moved by any sentiment when we arrive at the conclusion that divine healing is a blessing that has been provided by the Lord Jesus Himself. Once again we repeat that faith must be founded upon evidence and must be grounded on something that is strong enough to nourish it and to sustain it.

When we consider the ground work of our faith when it comes to the healing of the body, every poor sufferer should shout for joy. It is the shout that brings the victory. It is the anthem of joy that will make the walls fall down. It would be wonderful indeed were we to pray for physical deliverance, basing our prayer upon some promise of the Word of God. There is a sense in which we do that. But it is far more wonderful to believe that we can appropriate our physical healing because it has already been purchased for us through the atoning ministry of Jesus.

Divine healing is undoubtedly an integral part of the atoning work of the Lord Jesus Christ. Next time you meet around that sacred table with your brethren who form the body of your church—which is the Body of Christ—I want you to ask yourselves solemnly and sincerely a few very important questions. Why did Jesus differentiate between the wine and the bread? Why did He say, "This is My blood" and then again, "This is My body"? If the blood was shed for the remission of sins was there any need for the body to be broken for the same cause? It was a statement of Jesus that the blood was shed for them, and in addition to that, the body was broken for them.

The word that is in the very heart and core of the meaning of the atonement is the word *substitutional.* From Genesis to Revelation the Bible rings in type and anti-type with the declaration of this glorious truth. Why is it that I shall live eternally? Because Jesus died my death. Why is it that I can walk in holiness before Him? Because He took all of my sins. Why is it that I am redeemed and saved from the guilt of iniquity? Because Jesus not only bore my guilt and carried my sins in the judgment hall of Pontius Pilate, but He carried them before the tribunals of God.

Why is it that we are instructed in the Word by the apostle Paul to rejoice in the Lord? Because Jesus carried *all* of our grief. Why is it that we are instructed not to be anxious about the things of the present? Because He lifted our anxiety and gave us His promises for the future.

As He took my sin, He gave me His sinlessness. When He assumed my guilt He gave me His holiness. Beloved, the whole super-structure of the doctrine of the atonement would crumble if you took out of the foundation those two glorious words *substitutional* and *vicarious.* It must of necessity follow then that if substitution is a cardinal doctrine of the atonement as regards deliverance from sin, it must also be an essential doctrine with regard to deliverance from disease. In other words—if it is true that Jesus carried our sins in atoning for them, then He must of necessity have carried our sicknesses too, if He was going to atone for them in the same way.

One thing is very sure—if healing is not in the atonement then the Christian can only pray for it as a privilege; but if it is in the atonement he can claim it as a heritage. If it is not in the atonement the question of healing becomes a matter of intercession. If it is in the atonement it becomes a matter of appropriation. How can anybody appropriate without *faith*? By no stretch of the imagination would it be possible for anybody to become the recipient of the blessing except by *faith*.

You tell me that God could just give it to you without any exercise of faith on your part? That is what a great many people expect God to do. But He does not work that way. If He did that, would you ever seek His face? Would you ever pray? Would you ever draw away from the humdrum of this world and alone in your closet lift your hands to God? Some of you would not even take the trouble to read your Bible—and if God would visit you with health and heal your sickness, you would not even stop to thank Him for it. I know human nature well enough to be able to make that statement.

A man once contradicted a similar statement I made. He declared that under no circumstances would there be a human being on the face of the earth that would be ungrateful enough as not to thank the Lord if he became the recipient of such a blessing as that. I had dinner with that same man and he never took the time to thank the Lord for the food. As I passed him the bread and potatoes I told him that I was giving him two miracles of God's genius and power. He told me that he grew the potatoes and bought the bread—but what could he have done without God? During the conversation I unfolded the message that God brought to my heart while walking around in his grassy fields.

In that pasture were horses, cows, chickens, pigs, and sheep. They were all eating the same grass. They were all drinking the same water. The same identical water and food was somehow changed to strength in the horse, milk in the cow, eggs in the chicken, wool on the back of the sheep and bacon in the pigs. I then asked my friend if he did not think that was a miracle. He answered that it was nature. But back of what we call the natural is the supernatural. Back of the created is the Creator. To have one you must have the other. He then admitted that it was a miracle. God was behind the food on the table, the clothes on his back, the wood with which his house was built. He was even the Giver of the water that was in the glass by his side. Then I asked him why he did not thank God for them. He made no reply. But there will come a day when he will answer that question.

Chapter 12

Faith Is the Victory

*T*here are countless millions who receive the blessings of God just as a matter of fact. Because of His mercy He sends the rain upon the just and the unjust, and the grain of the sinner germinates just as quickly as the wheat of the saint. That is part of God's nature.

The manifestation of love is so profound that even the angels must stand in wonderment in contemplation of it. If man would take those things as a matter of course I am convinced that they would take any other spiritual or physical gift in exactly the same way.

So it is that God has designed this means of faith as the medium by which the things we hoped for become real, and the things He has promised become our possession.

In a word, I am convinced that in the matter of divine healing the problem is one of appropriation more than it is a problem of intercession. A man can intercede when his heart is unclean but he cannot appropriate until his heart has been made right with God. He might know how to ask, but he does not know how to receive! He has not yet discovered that faith is the victory. This is the victory that overcometh the world—even our faith.

The faith that is based upon the promises made to the redeemed children of God is intensified when we consider that it is based upon something that has *already been purchased.*

Paul in writing to the Corinthian Church very clearly and distinctly differentiates between the shed blood and the broken body of the Lord Jesus. The Corinthians were in grievous error regarding the celebration of the Lord's Supper. They were undoubtedly eating and drinking to excess. They were eating to satisfy their hunger and drinking to quench their thirst. Paul called them to shame when he declared, "What? have ye no houses to eat and drink in? or despise ye the church of God, and shame them that have not?" He also declared that they had missed the mark. He told them that they did not understand why the Lord's Supper was ever instituted. In First Corinthians 11:24 he declares that Jesus said, "Take, eat: this is My body, which is broken for you: this do in remembrance of Me."

Up to this time there had been no mention whatever of the bread. He did not join these two together and say, "These *things* do in remembrance of Me," but he segregated and separated them. He said "*This* do in remembrance of Me." By all the rules of logic this could only mean one thing. The body meant one thing and the blood meant another.

In First Corinthians 11:29-30 we find Paul's position with regard to the meaning of the broken body. He declared that some of the Corinthians were weak and sick and others were asleep. That meant that they were dead before their time. He emphatically declares that the reason was that they did not discern the Lord's body. In plain twentieth-century language this is what is meant, "Many of you members in the church at Corinth are sick and weak in your bodies and many of your members have died because you have not believed or understood that Jesus Christ bore your sicknesses."

What that church should have done was to have spent the same amount of energy in drawing near unto the Lord as they did in quarreling about the virtues of their various leaders and indulging in the sin of sectarianism that was dividing the Body of Christ. They could have been healed, but they discerned not the truth. Some who were dead could have been alive if they had only availed themselves of the privilege of the atonement.

The prophet of the captivity, Isaiah, turned the telescope down the vista of the years and foretold with minute accuracy the physical events regarding the atoning work of Jesus. He foresaw and foretold the spiritual application regarding His suffering and death. He declared that He was bruised for our iniquities. What is that but substitution? He states that He was wounded for our transgression. It is the statement of the vicarious nature of His atoning work. When the chastisement of our peace was upon Him, that was substitutional. Then he declares with emphasis that with His stripes we are healed.

He did not use the future tense—he did not use adjectives that befog the clear and plain statement of fact. Could anything be shorter, plainer, more forceful, easier to understand—than these words, "*By His stripes we are healed*"?

Matthew chapter 8 completely knocks the props out of the argument of the man who declares that means spiritual healing. It means nothing of the sort. It relates only to physical healing. It is undoubtedly tied up with the healing of the soul and the forgiveness of sins, because both are in the heart of the atonement. Matthew 8 records the healing of Peter's wife's mother, many who were possessed with devils, and all the sick that were brought to Jesus. Then it declares that these things occurred that it might be fulfilled which was spoken by Isaiah when he said, "Himself took our infirmities and bare our sicknesses" (Mt. 8:17).

Many opponents of divine healing have written to me and declared that Isaiah's prophecy was fulfilled then. What happened the next day and the next year, they inferred, could never be associated with the statement of the prophet. That argument is false because he was talking about one atoning work. There are not two atonements. There is only one. Half of the atonement cannot fall and the other half stand.

To me, friends, the glorious and eternal truth remains, in spite of everything that has been done and said against it, *your healing has been paid for.* Yes, paid for, by the Son of the living God Himself.

Why did they whip Him at the cruel post of scourging? Why did they bare His back and allow that Roman lash to descend upon Him? What stripes was it that Isaiah beheld through the lens of his telescope, and that make him declare under the power of the Spirit that with those stripes we are healed? Would a loving Father, beholding the culmination of the purpose for which He sent His Son into the world, permit Him to undergo agony and pain such as that if it were not for some purpose? The answer is obvious to every man and woman who will read the Scriptures with an open and unbiased mind.

By what authority did the disciples heal subsequent to the ascension of Jesus? Have you ever noticed the type of faith that they possessed when they came in contact with devils and with sickness? When they saw the man who was at the beautiful gate of the temple, they did not start to cry in sorrow and then lead him off to some place to intercede for God to have mercy upon him and bring healing to his body. To me they acted *as if they knew the mind of the Lord* in the matter. To me they acted like men who had come from direct contact with God in the power house of the upper room and they were sure that God Himself had power over sickness.

It was not intercession. *It was faith.* They did not claim that it was done by their power. They certainly acted like men who believed that Jesus had already done it. Using the name that is above every name they simply told him to get up and walk. That is just what the man did.

In plain words the thing that impresses me when I read the account—and the same truth is impressed upon me when I read every account of divine healing subsequent to the ascension of Jesus—is that they acted as if they believed and knew that healing *was in the atonement.*

Now what has all this to do with faith? It has a great deal to do with the subject of faith because it is upon this great truth that faith must stand when it operates in appropriating healing for the body.

There is a great deal of difference between the prayer of supplication and the victorious shout of faith. One leads to the other undoubtedly. Supplication might cry out of its need without being aware of any promises on which to stand, but faith knows its ground and reaches up to receive.

Are you sick in body, my friend? Do you need the deliverance that only God can give? Have faith in God. Have faith in His Word. Faith is the victory!

Remember that faith cometh by hearing and hearing by the Word of God. Walk hand in hand with the Spirit down the corridors of revealed truth as you turn over the pages of the inspired Word. There is no force under Heaven that can so quickly drive out the enemies of unbelief like the reading of the Word of God. Like Philip in the chariot of the eunuch helping the man to understand is the Holy Spirit who always accompanies the Word itself and unfolds it to the mind of the man who reads. As you read, the Word will grow on you—the promises will stand out—and you will begin to cry, "It is mine."

As the sinner appropriates salvation by faith, so the sick will appropriate their healing. God cannot lie. He must vindicate His own Word. He *must* abide by the thing He has promised to do. Heaven and earth may pass away, but the Word of the Lord will remain forever. When even the rocks and the mountains melt in fervent heat, the Rock of Ages that was cleft for me will still be seen in its manifested impregnability gracing and beautifying eternity. Could you ask for a more sure foundation than that?

When the prayer of intercession is over—when the tears of supplication have been shed—stand upon the promises and hold God to His Word. Your weeping may endure for a night, but joy will come in the morning.

As Job traveled from the old burning house to the new one he did not make the journey with a hop, skip, and jump. Just what time elapsed we do not know. But we do know that it was faith that held him steady through every experience of the test.

As one who can say in humility that I have seen thousands of people restored in body by the miraculous and marvelous healing power of God, I beseech you who are suffering to turn your eyes from yourself and the beggarly things of time. Lift them toward the face of One who has not only the nail prints in His hands but with whose stripes you are healed.

If you are tested, if you are being tried—keep turning over the pages of the treasure book of the Bible and as you read the promises of God keep saying within your heart, "Jesus never fails."

There is healing for you because Jesus purchased it. Remember the promise—yours—yours—Jesus purchased it. Remember the promise is yours—your promise—yours—yours. Commence to rejoice in it, praise God for it, hold that Bible to your heart—and sing, and sing again, "*Jesus never fails!*"

Chapter 13

Faith and Works

We now come to a study of the relationship between faith and works. That there is such relationship there is not the slightest doubt. James 2:20 declares that faith without works is dead. He tells us in that very remarkable and wonderful chapter that faith is something more than intellectual assent or even belief with the heart.

Faith not only believes, *but it does.* James declares that the devils believe; his inference is that if faith is nothing more than belief, then it would be possible to say that the devils have faith. But faith accomplishes things. You can have belief without accomplishment. I can say that there is an airplane leaving the local airport tonight at 8:00 for Chicago, but the fact that *I believe it* will not take me to the great metropolis in Illinois.

One of the troubles with the modern church is that it has some belief with no faith. There is belief in faith undoubtedly, but belief has to be moved into action before it can increase to appropriating faith. You can prove your faith by what you do; faith will prove itself by making you what you ought to be.

Faith must have a body. It must of necessity express itself and as it expresses itself it must be in works. There is always action to it. It is living, vitalized, moving, appropriating. It pulsates with activity—it is vibrant with spiritual life.

Let us examine for a little while some of the concrete cases that are recorded in Hebrews 11, the great faith chapter of the Bible.

The first incident that is given is the one of the elders obtaining a good report. If you will turn to the story of the Exodus, you will discover that there is no mention at all of the word *faith* in connection with their report. Paul is declaring that they showed their faith by *what they did*.

We next read of the faith of Abel offering unto God a more excellent sacrifice than that of Cain. But when we turn to Genesis 4 and read the account, we find that the word *faith* is never mentioned. Once again Paul is declaring that what Abel had when he offered his sacrifice unto the Lord was faith. He showed it by *what he did*. The sacrifice that was offered by Cain and brought such displeasure to the Lord was undoubtedly the product of the reasoning of this sinful man. Abel proved his faith by what he did, although no mention is made of faith as such in the Old Testament account.

We read in Hebrews 11:5 that by faith Enoch was translated that he should not see death, but in reading the very short account of the life of Enoch we discover that the word *faith* was never mentioned in connection with him at all. He, as we all know, is the type of those saints who are to be translated before the apocalyptic judgments. He lived in a day of iniquity and wickedness. He lived in a time of unbelief. In spite of every environment and circumstance the Scripture declares that he walked with God. One day he went for a walk and forgot to come back. The Bible declares he was not, for God took him. Paul, in his Epistle to the Hebrews, makes the emphatic declaration that *what he did* was faith. It was not only what he believed alone that made it faith, it was what that belief grew into when it was energized by activity. Faith must express itself—it must have a body—it must be in action.

We now come to Noah. He is another in the good parade of Old Testament worthies whom Paul brings out of the historical past as an example of faith before the eyes of the Hebrews of his day. You can read through the account of the building of the ark and the coming of the flood (see Gen. 6–9) and you will find absolutely no mention of *faith*. What the Lord does say to old Noah is, "For thee have I seen righteous before Me in this generation." In spite of the jeers of his friends and the criticism of the apostles of reason he went ahead in obedience to the Word of the Lord and built his ark. Thousands of years later Paul wrote to the Hebrews and said that that was faith.

And so he goes on reminding a race that was befogged and lost in the midst of its own doubts and fears of the faith of their forefathers in generations gone by. He tells them that these men exercised faith before they even had received the promises in the sense the Hebrews of Paul's day had become the recipients of the promises of God.

There is not the slightest doubt but what the teaching of both James and Paul is that faith, to be faith, *must be in action.* In order to accomplish something you must do something. How in the world could you ever accomplish anything unless you did the thing that you accomplished, or at any rate subscribed towards its consummation. So it is with faith.

Faith acts—it does something—it moves out. Its power increases as we use it. The little stream that flows today might become an irresistible river tomorrow, but it can never become a river if it were to be confined in the banks of a pool. To hide the talent in a napkin and bury it in the ground will never increase it; instead, rust is liable to destroy the treasure you think you possess. So the talent of faith if hidden and buried will begin to decay into inanimate belief and ultimately deteriorate and destroy itself by inactivity.

Put faith in action. Faith that builds the ark before the flood waters come will live to see the vindication of the divine word.

Faith that moves forward, that marches around the walls of Jericho with the elastic step of victory and the bugle notes of triumph, will smash down the walls of Jericho every time.

Faith that never looks back, that takes an Abraham on a road of unknown future, will perhaps bring blessings to the heart, as God sent seed to the Patriarch, as numberless as the sands of the sea. He gave up the present for the future—he said "Goodbye" to the things he had for what was promised.

Faith in testing, such faith as inspired Daniel when they lead him to the lions' den, will open the doors of the palaces of the king and frustrate the purposes of the enemies of God.

Faith on the march goes onward one step at a time, even though the wheels of Pharaoh's chariot might be rumbling in the rear and the seemingly impassible Red Sea be not far ahead. But the faith that marches on will always sit on the hillside of victory and listen to some Miriam and her maidens sing a song of deliverance while they play their tambourines of praise.

So it is that James asked the question, "You say you have faith? What are you doing with it?" He wants to know. If you tell him you are doing nothing, that you just have faith and that it never accomplishes anything—never gets any results—then the apostle declares it is dead.

But when you tell him that you have faith and that faith works because you work your faith, then James is willing to praise the Lord with you. The way to prove that faith works is to work your faith. Give it a body—put it in action—wait not for a ton but use the ounce that God has given you. Before a man can be ruler over many cities he has to prove himself faithful over one. But if he locks up the gate of the city that God has given him and the inhabitants of the soul sleep in apathy and in lethargy, he will never become a George Müller and will never know the power of active, appropriating faith.

On the foundation of God's Word I stand when I declare unto you that all things—not some things—but *all things* are possible to the man who believes.

When we pray we should ask in faith, and in that faith there should not be an element of doubt. All things are possible to the man who believes—because when he believes, he believes God. Jesus is the author and finisher of our faith.

Chapter 14

Conclusion

*T*hus it is we find ourselves at the conclusion of this book, but by no means at the end of the glorious possibilities of acting, appropriating faith. All books must have a conclusion—but faith can have none. It might have its beginning in time—but its effect will be heralded along the vaulted corridors of eternity.

So it is that I climb in the spirit the Pisgah Mountain of my experience and gaze with wondering eyes across the Jordan into the realms of the eternal and the infinite. I see them marching—stalwarts of faith, heroes of the cross—marching in triumph and singing the song of the victor.

The night has passed—eternal day has broken. No longer do they walk around the walls of some Jericho that has to be taken—but they march in victory within the walls of a city whose builder and maker is God. No longer do they blow the bugles for the walls to fall down—they rather blow the golden trumpets of joy because every wall has fallen and there are no more walled cities to conquer. Theirs is the song of the victor. Theirs is the anthem of triumph.

They are all there, those heroes of faith: Abraham and Isaac and Jacob; Daniel and Ezekiel and Joel—and all the worthies whose names scintillate like gems from the open page of the eleventh chapter to the Hebrews.

They are all there, those who lived and died in faith: Peter and James and Paul and Silas and Timothy, together with those who fired the world with the gospel message in the days when the memory of the cross was fresh and the touch of the Savior's hand had not been forgotten.

They are all there, those worthies of the reformation: Luther and Tyndall and Latimer; Knox and Calvin and Whitfield, joining their voices with the ancient patriarchs in singing the song of Moses and the Lamb.

They are there, those champions of the faith of our fathers: Wesley and Spurgeon and Booth, together with the millions that worshiped in the church at Philadelphia, whose garments were unspotted by the world.

Methinks as I turn the ear of the spirit away from the noise and din of a world that has lost its faith, that I can hear them singing, praising, shouting, chanting where the waters of the glassy sea murmur a celestial hymn of praise. The song that was begun on earth shall never be finished even in Heaven. Eternity is a long time during which the redeemed of all ages can sing the songs that will make the angels wonder: "Faith was the victory...faith was the victory...that overcame the world."

This book must have an end, but there will be no end to faith! If you would enjoy that never ending participation in the song of triumph there, you must not forget while you are down here that "This is the victory that overcometh the world, *even our faith.*"

Part Two

The Sick Are Healed

Dedication

This book is prayerfully dedicated to the sick and suffering everywhere. It contains some of the cream of the author's sermons and writings, as well as a number of testimonies, all blended together that it might be an instrument in the hands of God in pointing the sick to the healing Christ.

The author has endeavored to imagine himself seated in a chair by your side. He has endeavored to anticipate your problems—to feel your heartthrobs and to bring you the message that you need in your hour of testing. He has prayed earnestly that this book might find its way into hospitals and sick rooms and that the Holy Spirit will reveal the truth of the Word divine as its pages are read.

The author hopes that it will be used by the saints of God everywhere as a silent minister to the sick and needy. Written and sent forth in prayer, it is dedicated to all those who would know experimentally the glorious truth: "He was wounded for our transgressions, He was bruised for our iniquities...and with His stripes we are healed."

Chapter 15

The Sick Are Healed

I am so sorry you are sick. I am writing this book for you—writing it in prayer that God will lay His healing hand upon you and that like the poor sufferers in the days of old, you too will receive a visit from the healing Christ.

Perhaps you are wondering what there will be in this book—whether or not there is some trick or catch somewhere. No, my dear friend, there is nothing to send for, nothing to pay, for the healing power of our Lord and Savior Jesus Christ is as free as salvation for our guilty souls, and the air we breathe day by day. I believe the Bible to be the inspired Word of God, and I believe that in that Holy Book there is clear and glorious teaching that in the days in which we live the sick can be healed by the power of the Great Physician.

I want you to read it carefully, thoughtfully and prayerfully. Will you not ask, with me, that the Holy Spirit will illumine your mind and heart as you read? Whoever you are, wherever you are, I pray that you will be conscious of One by your side with nail prints in His hands. He was wounded for your transgressions and with His stripes you are healed.

To you who are well and who do not need the healing touch of our Lord, I make the appeal that you will join me in earnest prayer that the power of the Lord Jesus may be as manifest on the earth today as it was when He was here to walk and talk with men. Remember that prayer changes things. Do not forget that by praying for others you will receive the Father's blessing on your own life.

More than once I have found that my own burdens have been lifted when I have prayed about the sorrows and cares of others. We are instructed in the Scriptures to bear one another's burdens and in so doing we shall fulfill the law of Christ; but more than that we shall sit down in our Father's palace at the banqueting table of love and grace.

I am firmly and thoroughly convinced that we are living in the closing days of time. I also believe the devil knows it. I am certain that he is doing everything he can to impede the children of the Lord in their homeward journey toward their heavenly goal. He is using every weapon at his command. The devils of doubt and of fear, of sickness and of disease, have been sent forth not only to trouble the children of sin but also to fasten themselves upon the children of the Lord.

It was not to unsaved people that the words were spoken, "Resist the devil and he will flee from you," but it was to children of light who knew and loved Christ.

Chapter 16

What Is Divine Healing?

*F*irst of all let us answer the question: "Is there any such thing as divine healing?" Without hesitancy we declare that there is. We all know that in every human being we find the combination of two natures. We are soul and body, spirit and matter—yes, even Heaven and earth. We know and we believe that we are the direct creation of God Himself. To believe otherwise is not only preposterous and foolish from the natural standpoint, but it is an insult to God Himself from the spiritual side of our natures.

The very fact that we are a combination of matter and spirit—that we can walk the earth and yet commune with God—is in itself an unanswerable argument against our evolutionary development from the lower forms of life. No, my friend, God created us in His own image. It is not my purpose in this volume to attempt to prove the fall of man, for you can see the evidence on every hand and side.

It is my purpose, however, to prove to you that when the Redeemer came to restore us from the Fall, He came to bring redemption for the entire man; not for one-half of him or even three-fourths of him, but for man in his completeness, which embraces, of course, both soul and body. It is absolutely impossible to read the Bible with unprejudiced mind and not become convinced of this great and eternal fact.

It is not the body of man that sins. It is the spirit of man that is iniquitous. The body can feel the effects of sin and it does. The body can be made to become an instrument of sin only because of the iniquity of the mind and heart. Sin goes deeper than the physical manifestation. It is not only what you do that God looks at, but it is the thing in you that impells you to do it. It is what you are more than what you do. So it is we have a picture of fallen man—fallen in soul and fallen in body. Thus it is we have a photograph of God's human creation sick in spirit and sick in body.

God's Great Love

Then there came a glorious and marvelous day in the councils of Heaven. Because "God so loved the world" and because His great divine heart looked in pity and compassion upon men who had gotten themselves into this pitiful condition—it was because of these things, I say, the Lamb of God was sent to die an atoning death on Calvary's cross.

It is the teaching of the Word of the Lord that the death of Jesus purchased redemption for the complete man. Of that there can be no doubt. The day will dawn when the fullness of that glorious redemption will be made manifest.

Because I have mentioned the fact that the body can become the instrument of sin, it does not necessarily mean that every case of sickness is the direct result of sin in the life of the sick person.

The disciples evidently thought that was the case when they came to Jesus at one time and said, "Master, who did sin, this man or his parents that he was born blind?" Jesus very quickly put aside their arguments and thoughts in the answer that He gave. He stated that that case of blindness could not be attributed to sin in either of them. There was another reason for the blindness of that particular man.

Many of God's dearest and noblest children are sick. Many who have been walking in the light have been attacked by the adversary of their souls. Many of the dearest and sweetest saints I have ever known have been the target for the arrows of suffering that have left the bow of the devil. As a matter of fact, I am persuaded that sometimes it is because we do walk so close to the Lord that the devil tries to put infirmities upon us. You see, he wants to bring the work of the Lord into disrepute.

For some time I have felt the need for a reaffirmation of faith in the subject of divine healing. So many have been shaken by the continued visitation of disease and sickness and because of the multitude of physical sorrows that have come upon the face of the earth. Just as it is hard for a sinner to believe in salvation while he still lives in sin, it is also hard to maintain faith in healing when sickness confronts us on every hand and side.

We are in a fight. There is no doubt about that. Victories are not gained by borrowing the wings of angels and flying over the country without opposition from the devil. We have to battle for every foot of ground we gain. We have to fight and fight hard for the victory in these days of trial.

I pray God that the words that are to follow will not only anchor you in the faith that you have already received, but that your faith will multiply and increase as once again you hold high the Bible in the face of a frowning, unbelieving world. While the cold sands of adversity blow against your cheek, you can still hold aloft the Word of God and proclaim, "Though Heaven and earth shall pass away, God's Word still abides."

Healing Is Your Inheritance

The first thing that I want to emphasize is the fact that as children of the Lord, you have a right to claim divine healing as your inheritance.

If a rich man died and left you some property, both in money and in real estate, you would not hesitate to come forth and claim what belongs to you. You would get in touch with the administrator and you would be careful not to lose contact with the executor. You would not go forth with the spirit of one who is petitioning and begging for the portion of goods that had been left to you, but you would march forward boldly in faith to claim what was your portion. The question of whether you deserved it or not would not enter into the matter at all. As a matter of fact an inherited property is very seldom deserved.

When it comes to the question of divine healing, however, if we with unprejudiced minds would read the Word of God, we cannot arrive at any other conclusion but that the Lord left divine healing to His church in His last will and testament. He earned it, He purchased it, and He paid for it, and He told His church they could have it. He sent the Holy Spirit to become the administrator.

It is our privilege to carefully read the will and be persuaded in our own minds that it is our inheritance, and then get in contact with the Divine administrator of the testament and ask aid in the reception and *appropriation* of our inheritance. This fact must be clearly understood and this truth must be comprehended before we can become the possessors of the things our Lord has purchased.

It is the lack of recognition of this truth that lies behind the fact that so many Christians are sick and weakly in these days. If we doubt the fact that divine healing is our inheritance, then faith loses its power of appropriation and we stand helpless in the clutches of sickness and disease.

If what I say is true then it must necessarily follow that healing is for *all of God's children.* That is what I most emphatically declare. It is a tremendous hindrance to the faith of the Christian, when uncertainty crowds to the forefront of the mind and we begin to doubt whether or not it is God's will to heal at all.

We are persuaded that it is the will of the Lord to heal *some,* and we praise the Lord when we hear the testimony of the deliverance of others, but it is difficult for us to believe that it is the will of the Lord to heal us. When it becomes a personal matter, doubt commences to rise, and the conflict is on between faith and reason.

Every sufferer, who turns to the Lord for deliverance, must first become convinced that *it is God's will to heal him.* Unless you arrive at that conclusion, it is impossible for you to exercise faith. Not a sinner could ever be saved who knelt at the altar and doubted the will of the Lord regarding the salvation of his soul. He writes the pardon on my heart the moment I believe. Faith begins to grow in the garden of the heart when we know we are in the will of the Lord.

Chapter 17

Is Healing for All?

*I*f it is the will of the Lord to heal *some,* and not to heal others, then not a soul in the world would have any real basis for faith. It would take a special manifestation of divine power, or a special revelation of God's will to assure you that you were among those who had been chosen by God to be the recipient of healing.

Remember these facts! Faith must be based upon God's will. It would be impossible to exercise faith unless you knew that the promises of God were given to you. I want to remind you also that faith is only imparted and anointed by the Holy Spirit when it operates *within the revealed* will of God. Outside of the divine will there may be desire or supplication, but there could not be a divinely imparted faith. We must arrive at the inevitable conclusion that it is God's will to heal us—and that healing is for us all.

I presume at this point somebody will raise the objection that if we follow this teaching to its logical conclusion, it means that we shall never die. Such an attitude would be a perversion of Scripture! Divine healing has never gone any *farther* than the promises of God. Faith must be based upon His promise—and there is not a promise in the Word that declares that we shall never die. God has the power to take us by the translated route to the realms of Glory, but He has not promised to do so until the Son of Man appears in the clouds on that great triumphant day.

The Word of the Lord declares that the days of our years are three score and ten. In Exodus 23:25-26, He says, "...I will take sickness away from the midst of thee...the number of [the] days I will fulfill." The saint of God does not shun death. To him it is a portal through which he passes from a land of sorrow to an eternity of never fading joy. He does not shrink from the thought of casting away the robes of mortality and being clothed with the garments of holiness and immortality.

Paul was in a strait twixt two opinions. He could not decide which would be better—to stay here and preach or to be with the Lord. He certainly did not pray to be delivered from death, but he *did* pray to be healed from his sickness. If you have been stumbling over the fact that if it is God's will to heal, then death would never come—let me remind you once again that divine healing never goes any farther than the promises of God.

Jehovah-Rapha

Do you not remember that after the children of Israel had crossed the Red Sea, and they were delivered from the cruel hand of Pharaoh, it was to them—all of them—that the Lord made His covenant of healing?

If we are going to use that pilgrim journey as a type of the voyage of the Christian from earth to Heaven, why not use all of it? Why not take every bit of the type and then praise God for the harmonious way in which it fits into the anti-type?

Did God promise to heal only part of the people? No, He promised to heal them all. Did He tell them some would be healed more than others? No, He made a covenant that included all the men and women and children of the tribe—from Moses down to the smallest infant.

It is true that God made certain conditions, but when those conditions were met we read that there was not one feeble person among all the tribes. It was here that the glorious banner was unfurled that bore one of the redemptive names of the Lord. Jehovah-Rapha was emblazoned in letters of gold that all might read and rejoice. "I am the Lord that healeth thee," shouted the children of Israel.

The protecting power of God turned back from His chosen people the armies of sickness, pain, and disease. It was not until they got out of divine order—their covenant with God broken—that sickness overtook the tribe, and disease once again fastened itself upon them.

We can say today that *Jehovah-Rapha* means "I am the Lord that healeth thee." It is still *Jehovah-Rapha*: "I am the Lord that healeth thee."

Some day when you are discouraged, get your concordance and march across the highways of Bible history, up to the mountain peaks and through the valleys—through Old and New Testament promises and let those words *I AM* ring through the corridors of your souls. Over and over again they occur. The saint of God who receives them and believes them will shout it in the face of hell, and the enemy from the pit will flee in dismay. The eternal Son of God is the same yesterday, today, and forever. His banner over us is love, and we can still hear His words, "I am the Lord that healeth thee."

"A mighty fortress is our God,
A bulwark never failing;
Our helper He, amid the flood
Of mortal ills prevailing."[1]

The Ancient Type

Is healing for you? Is healing for all? The Word of the Lord declares it. Our faith cometh by hearing and hearing by the Word of the Lord.

Let us examine again the type of healing exemplified by the brazen serpent that was set up in the wilderness. Moses never would have thought of that. None of the tribes of Israel ever would have thought of that. None of the tribes of Israel ever would have dreamed of a system of healing so simple and so powerful as the one God devised. Upon that sun-baked plain there was placed aloft a serpent of brass that surmounted a high pole. The suffering people were told, on the authority of the revealed word of the Lord, that there was to be *life for a look* at the brazen serpent.

Remember that *everybody in the tribes* were included in the invitation. God could have looked down from the glory, and from the basis of compassion and mercy healed them all without the use of the serpent. But it is in God's economy that the element of faith must operate in the reception of healing power. If the sick man had insisted on staying indoors and had refused to look upon the brazen serpent, his sickness would have been unto death.

The Scripture tells us that every man, woman, and child—for the promise was for all—who looked upon the brazen serpent found healing at the hand of a compassionate God. The healing was not in the serpent— it was not in the look—the healing was the supernatural manifestation of God's power in bringing deliverance to their bodies. Don't forget that it was for them all.

There is still life for a look at the crucified One. As Moses raised the serpent in the wilderness, even so was the Son of God raised up, that people looking upon Him might not only be healed in soul, but healed in body. You must come to the place where you believe it is God's will to heal you, or I am afraid that your poor faith will not be strong enough to reach out and receive the blessing.

Endnote

1. "A Might Fortress Is Our God," lyrics by Martin Luther.

Chapter 18

One of the Greatest Miracles of Modern Times

[Mrs. Louis S. Johnston, Laurel, Ontario, Canada]

I think it would be well at this time for me to tell you a story—a narrative so seemingly incredible and so wonderful that it would be very hard for some to believe, were there no positive proof to substantiate it. After I had related this story in a great arena meeting a clergyman came to me and said, "If that story is true then it means that the day of miracles is not past. If that story is true, then we ministers have been missing some of the greatest opportunities for bringing Jesus to a needy world that Heaven itself has put in our hands."

Yes, my poor sick friend, this story is true. I think perhaps it would be better to have the person upon whom this miracle was performed tell you about it in her own words:

"How pleased I am to tell to others, how Jesus the Great Physician made me well, after my being a helpless cripple for over ten years. When I touched the hem of His garment He wrought a miracle in my body, just as He did in those who touched Him in the days of long ago.

"After three years of happy married life, I contracted tonsillitis, which turned to quinsy, then to rheumatic fever. I had three medical doctors and two trained nurses. The doctors hardly thought I would live through the rheumatic fever, I had such a heavy attack of it, but after being in bed 13 weeks, I gradually became sufficiently well to be up.

"However, the fever had left my [legs] in a very painful condition, and during that summer and fall, they became much worse, until they got so bad that I could not walk nor stand nor even move. Back to bed I had to go, and there I stayed for about three years, for I was not able even to sit in a chair. I was under the care of three medical doctors, who truly did all they could to help me, but nothing made me any better.

"Then we decided to try something else, so I was taken to Toronto (60 miles distant) where we spared no expense in trying to get something to make me well. We tried every remedy or doctor that we or our friends thought could give me any benefit. The next five years I was taken to Toronto frequently, and was under the care of doctors for sometimes four, six, eight or ten weeks at a time, then was brought home for a few weeks and taken back again. I had 20 different doctors, yes, doctors of all kinds—medical doctors, specialists, chiropractors, osteopaths, homeopaths, electric treatments, massage treatments, X-ray, etc., etc.

"I suffered greatly with my throat as well as my [legs]. At times for several weeks (one time 14) I could not speak a single word, even in a whisper. I had to make signs or write what I had to make known. The doctors took out my tonsils twice (five years' time between the operations), also operated on the back of my throat. Then I had all my teeth extracted as some of my physicians thought the teeth might be causing my trouble.

"All efforts were of no avail. Sometimes I would be slightly better only to become worse again. The doctors never claimed to be able to diagnose my disease correctly, as they declared I was an exceptional case. They believed as they declared, however, that my extreme pain was a combination of rheumatism and neuritis resulting from my severe attack of rheumatic fever. I suffered excruciatingly night and day, and had to be cared for like a baby.

"Although the greater part of my ten years' illness I was in bed, yet at intervals during the last seven years I was able to sit in a chair. My husband carried me wherever I had to be taken and when that became too hard on him we got two crutches but I never got well enough to use both of them, for my [legs] were too helpless. The lower part of my back was very painful also.

"Sometimes, when my husband would not be in the house to carry me, I would slide down off my chair onto the floor, and crawl to where I wanted to go. Oh no, I couldn't creep like a little child, but just sat on the floor, and with my two hands a little behind me, I would shove myself. It was a very painful piece of moving, and my hands became very sore, with hard calloused lumps on them. Both [legs] became very small and the right one got to be only about three-fourths the size of the left.

Untold Suffering

"The first three years of my affliction were spent in bed, the next five years mostly in Toronto, then the last two years I stayed home, although I still kept taking different kinds of treatments (electric and osteopathic) in our nearest town.

"Although, as I said before, I never got well enough to use the two crutches, yet, sometimes, (and it was only *sometimes*, for very often I could not bear even to be carried) I could go the length of the room, or a very short distance, by my husband lifting me up until my weight on the right side was on a crutch, and he himself supported me on the left side. My right [leg] would not straighten out, but was bent in sort of a crook behind the left one. In walking this way my right [leg] of course did not touch the floor by eight or ten inches, and the left one barely touched the floor. Almost my whole weight rested on my husband and crutch.

"The best that earthly aid could do for me, for those ten long years, was to keep me in bed or on a chair. Ten long years of misery and torture passed by, with suffering that could never be described, and then when we seemed to have come to the end of the road, there being nothing else to do or try, yes, then, we heard of, and came in touch with a Physician who never fails, even the Great Physician.

"Yes, one day, when my suffering was so intense that I could not even sit up, but was lying on a couch, too ill all over even to take notice of things, we heard that an evangelist, Dr. Price by name, was having meetings and praying for the sick people, many of whom became well.

"To make this part of my story short, I was taken to Paris, Ontario, Canada (70 miles away) where Dr. Price was holding a campaign. Although we knew nothing whatever of anything in this line, yet we were always willing and anxious to accept anything that might possibly help me. We reached Paris, October 15, 1924, in time for the evening meeting. On the following Sunday, October 19, Jesus touched my poor pain-racked body, and healed me instantly.

"How well I remember the evangelist's message that first night, how he told us, that 'He is able, He is willing and He will,' both for soul and body. 'Faith cometh by hearing and hearing by the Word of God,' and as I listened to the clear and powerful exposition of God's Word, as declared by the Lord's faithful servant Dr. Price, every bit of my very being did hunger for more of Jesus. It was Jesus, whom the evangelist exalted; Jesus, who was lifted up to draw all to Him. As I looked and beheld the blessed Christ of Galilee, I was indeed drawn to Him, and lost sight of the evangelist almost entirely.

"During my ten years' illness, my husband and I had prayed, oh yes, we prayed often, that the Lord would bless the means we were using to make me well. Truly we shed many bitter tears over my hopeless condition. We were members of the Methodist Church, and had both been brought up in Christian homes. Up to the time of our hearing God's Word given out in such a real and living way in those meetings, we were led to believe that the age of healing through prayer was over, and that all we poor sick and afflicted ones could do was to wait patiently until we would be called home.

"God was now opening His Word to us in larger way in these meetings and as He removed the scales from our eyes, we saw that the healing stripes that Jesus bore on the cross for the healing of our bodies, were just as real, as the cleansing blood He shed for the remission of our sins.

"When the first altar call was given, I asked my husband to take me to the altar and he picked me up in his arms and carried me to the altar, and laid me down beside it. No, I certainly could not kneel, neither could I sit, like other people, but had to lean against the bench in a reclining position. I don't think I missed being taken to the altar in any one of the meetings where an altar call was given. Oh how my heart was melted as I stayed by that altar bench; how I did cry to Jesus with a broken and a contrite heart. He showed me myself as I really was, and I can truly say that for a time, I lost sight of my need for my body, for I wanted Jesus most of all as my Savior. Yes, I wanted more of Jesus, I wanted the Blesser more than the blessing. I do praise Him that He drew me close, so very close to Him, and then, after consecrating my life to Him and making a full surrender, I asked Him to heal my afflicted body.

The Miracle

"At the close of the Sunday evening's service, after drinking in the glorious truths of God's Word in four days' meetings, I was again at the altar, and by faith kneeling at the foot of the old rugged cross I was so lost with Jesus, and so melted with His love, that I was scarcely conscious of preacher or people. Then, such an overpowering sweetness of the Holy Spirit came upon me that I became indeed completely dead to what was going on around me.

"Just then the Lord gave me such a precious vision of the straight and narrow way—a vision that has stayed with me ever since, for He showed me that the narrow way was the way in which I must walk. At this time the evangelist obeyed the command in God's Word, James 5:14, and offered prayer for the healing of my body, after which, I then sat upon the bench. Someone offered to get my crutch, as the time had now come to leave the building, but I said, "No, I do not need any crutch tonight." Then my husband went to lift me up, but I said "No" again.

"Oh, I just *knew* that Jesus would not fail me, if I trusted Him fully. (Anyone not knowing what I suffered, could not realize what it meant for me even to make an effort to move, for any extra moving meant additional pain, and would probably necessitate my having to go to bed for days or weeks.) However, I had come to the place where I believed the Word *absolutely*, praise God, and believed too that the present time was the time to trust Him completely, and to depend on Him alone to enable me to walk.

"To this day, I do not know how I arose to my feet, but Jesus gave me the faith to try, and then He did the rest. Up to that very moment, the pain was just as severe, (many times during the meetings I could not keep the tears back, for the pain was so hard to bear) but the very instant that I was on my feet, *I had not an ache nor a pain.* Glory to His precious name!

"My poor twisted [leg] became straight, and both [legs] received power to walk *immediately*, and I walked alone, with Jesus, unaided by any earthly help whatever. The prisoner had been loosed, the captive set free in a moment's time, by the mighty power of Jesus. And, wonder of wonders, the next time I looked at my [legs] they were *exactly the same size*. I could tell no difference.

"As I walked I did not know my feet were touching the floor, for I seemed to be walking in the air. Yes, I walked the full length of the big arena, (my husband by my side) then up the street to where our car was parked, opened the car door myself, and got in the car myself.

"My crutch had been left behind, in the arena, where it was hung in full view on the platform, for everyone to see what the Lord had done. Hundreds of people followed us out to the street and to the car, and I think most of them were weeping and praising God for beholding such a mighty miracle. I myself was not conscious of very much besides Jesus, and that He had made me to walk. That night I knew what it was to sleep soundly all night, and to turn myself without pain, for the first time in ten years.

"What a Great Physician! Yes, it was He who performed the miracle, not Dr. Price, the evangelist. It was Dr. Price who showed me the way, by his faithful preaching of the Word (may God bless him) and it was the blessed Word that got down into my heart and was made real.

"Have I been able to walk ever since that night Jesus touched me and made me completely well (my very bad throat was healed as well as my [legs]); has the healing lasted? Yes, Praise God! My healing has lasted. I am so glad to witness that the same Jesus who has power to save and to heal, is also able to keep and He has kept me, all glory to Him!

"Dear ones who are sick in either body or soul, oh I just plead with you to let Jesus have His way in your lives. There is no one so able, no one so willing as He, for every need. He has paid a costly price, even the shedding of His precious blood, to purchase freedom from sin and sickness for all who will believe. What He asks of us, is not silver nor gold, but that our lives might be wholly yielded unto Him.

"All that I need He will always be,
All that I need till His face I see,
All that I need through eternity,
Jesus is all I need."

That, my friends, is the story of a modern miracle, a story that should enable you to lift your hands in faith toward Heaven and touch the robe of the healing Christ. He is near you now and His truth has not lost its healing power.

Chapter 19

The Walk of Obedience

*G*od is no respecter of persons. He does not choose *some* to be the recipients of grace that He withholds from *others.* The thought then crops into your mind that God gives to some more than He does to others. Is that not because some live nearer to the heart of God? Is that not because some walk the road of obedience, and walking in the light today means that they will be given more light tomorrow?

The promises of God that are fulfilled in one man's life *can* be fulfilled in another. If we do not receive we cannot blame the Lord. We must ask Him to turn the searchlight of truth upon our own hearts. It may be that the prayer of consecration and surrender to His will will reveal to us the hindering cause buried within the confines of our flesh. It is true we cannot pay for our healing by our good works and our righteousness, but we can hinder and prevent it by our refusal to walk in all the light of God.

If healing were for the man next door and not for you, then God would be a respecter of persons. He never asks us to do the impossible, but He does demand of us that we walk in the light that streams from Heaven upon the pathway that He would have you travel.

"My life is in Thy hands," I cried,
Yet day by day, my plans I tried
To put in action; always feeling
Thy will for me Thou wert concealing.
And then one day, Thy Word I read:
"Thy will, not mine, be done," it said;
And, "He who wills to know My way
Shall know the Truth from day to day."

For many years I did not understand the meaning of the statement in Psalm 107:20a, "He sent His word, and healed them." That does not mean that the priest stood behind the sacred desk, and as the Word of the Lord was read, it brought healing to all the diseased and sick. The power was not in the mere reading of the sacred Scripture, by the lips of the priest. It meant that the people *received* the Word, they *digested* it, they *assimilated* it, they walked in the light of it, and because they did these things they found healing for soul and body.

That Word was an inspiration to their faith; that Word was an illuminator of the will of God; that Word was the voice of God giving His merciful promises to a needy people. His Word rolled out over the congregation a veritable ocean of the love and compassion and mercy of the divine heart, and people found healing because they *received the Word* of the Lord.

Let me remind you that the Scripture does not say that He sent forth the Word and healed some of them, but it included everybody. It declares He sent forth His Word and healed them all.

He Healed Them All

As we walk with our blessed Lord along the highways of service as revealed by the Gospels, over and over again we come across the fact that He healed them all.

Matthew chapter 4 gives us a glorious description of the ministry of the healing Christ in the province of Galilee. The Scriptures tell us that great multitudes of people followed Him. They came not only from Galilee but also from Decapolis, from Jerusalem and Judea, and from the other side of the Jordan. Moffatt, in his translation, declares He healed them all.

In Matthew 9 the word *all* occurs over and over again. It states that He healed every sickness and every disease among the people. Beholding the burdened, pain-wracked multitude, Matthew declares He was so moved with compassion that He not only healed them himself but He imparted to His disciples the power to go out into the villages and bring healing to the people who lived therein. They were told to heal all manner of disease and all manner of sickness.

Matthew declares again in chapter 12 that great multitudes followed the healing Christ as He tried to withdraw Himself from the people. Once again He healed them. Yonder He beheld a great multitude and again, "moved with compassion," the Scripture declares that He healed them all (see Mt. 14:14).

The question naturally arises in your mind as to why all are not healed today, when they were all healed in the days of Jesus under His personal ministry? My answer to that question is this: if the Lord Jesus were to enter your church some Sunday morning in person with His nail-pierced hands and His bleeding feet, I believe everybody who is sick would be inspired with such confidence and assurance and faith that the healing waters would flow over the entire congregation.

More than once at our healing meetings in the great campaigns, I have noticed when some outstanding miracle of healing has occurred, faith commences to roll like a river until the power of God has fallen upon the whole congregation. Our wonderful Jesus is still the healing Christ and the promises are just as good today as they were in the days of the long ago.

"If Thou Canst Believe"

Let me call your attention to the healing of the devil-possessed boy at the foot of the mount of transfiguration. Let me draw the picture upon the canvas of your mind.

Yonder stands a weeping father, heartbroken because of this terrible devil that has taken possession of his child. Over yonder writhing on the ground, thrown around by the demon of epilepsy, is the boy.

Around him stand the disciples shouting at the top of their voices, "In the name of Jesus I command you to come out of him." I can see them as their faces grow red in the intensity of their prayer. Louder and louder they command the devil to come out of him. How long they prayed we do not know. It might have been a matter of minutes, or it might have been a matter of hours.

I can visualize curious throngs that have gathered to watch the proceedings. Perhaps some Pharisee is there with a sickening grin on his face. Maybe that man over there has a sneer upon his countenance. Perhaps someone in the crowd is saying, "It is not God's will to heal him." Someone else declares, "This is a punishment for sin." Some of these things are matters of conjecture, but we do know that the disciples of the Lord, in spite of their direct contact with Jesus, were unable to bring healing to that boy.

Then something happened. Down the mountainside comes Jesus Himself. The poor grief-stricken, anxious father's faith had evidently begun to ebb out when he saw the failure of all of those gospel preachers that were doing their best, and yet they were failing in the task. Perhaps the devil had whispered to him that it was not God's will to heal his son. We do not know. We do know that he saw Jesus. When men see Jesus everything begins to change. When that Personality walks across the pathway of your life you have a right to believe that there is going to be a transformation.

That poor brokenhearted father rushed up to Him, and throwing himself at His feet said, "If Thou canst do anything, have compassion!" Listen to those words, "*If Thou canst.*" "*If Thou* canst." "If *Thou canst.*"

The Master looked at him with tender, compassionate eyes. Then He declared, "If *thou canst believe, all* things are possible to [them] that [believe]." Think of that statement, my friend. What was Jesus declaring? He was stating in no uncertain terms that it was His will. The question was forever settled regarding the fact of it being His will. That was not the thing that hindered. The thing that was hindering was the lack of faith on the part of the men who prayed and on the part of the father himself. There might have been some lack of faith too on the part of the boy at the moment when he was rational.

This truth stands out prominently that the failure of the disciples to cast out the devil was not because it was the will of the Lord that he should remain sick. It was because of a lack of faith on the part of the people who should have possessed it. That is why the Lord turned this man's statement completely around and made him declare that the hindering cause was not the lack of divine will, but the lack of faith in humanity to believe that will.

"According to Your Faith"

The poor father sensed this. Out of his heart came the agonizing cry, "Lord, I believe; help Thou mine unbelief."

What a picture to make angels and men rejoice! Jesus stood by that boy in all the majesty of His regal deity. The boy himself saw Him and looked into the eyes that were divine. The devil in the boy saw Him and began to tremble. The crowds saw Him and the Scripture says that they came running together. From this statement I infer that they had begun to disperse. They might have gone away muttering their maledictions against God and ridiculing divine healing. They might have held the disciples up to ridicule and scorn. They had failed. There was no doubt about that. But when Jesus stepped onto the scene it was altogether different. The Lord Himself rebuked that evil spirit and commanded that deaf and dumb spirit to come out of him and enter no more into him.

I do not know whether the people were astonished or not, but I do know that the evil spirit in that boy began to crawl out. The devil was mad. He always is mad when God makes him let go of one of His children. That evil spirit acted like some robber who was giving his victim a kick before he walked away. He rent him sore, but just the same, in obedience to the Word of the Lord *he had to come out.*

The boy lay there like one dead. He was flat on his back, he was prostrate before the Lord. They did not say he was hypnotized. No, they left that for the Pharisees of today. They declared, however, that he was dead. I presume that the boy was lying there exhausted after the terrific conflict with the evil spirit who had possessed him.

Let me say that there are generally physical manifestations accompanying the healing power of Jesus. I believe in real devils, but hallelujah, I believe in a real Christ and He is greater than them all.

Then the Master stooped down and took the boy by the hand, raised him up and gave him to his rejoicing father. The wonderful narrative closes by recording that the amazed disciples looked into the face of the Master and said, "Why, Master, could we not cast that devil out?" The reply was, "This kind cometh out only by fasting and prayer."

This is a tremendous lesson. What seemed to be failure before Jesus came, was not the fact that it was not God's will to heal him, but it was the fact that a faithless generation did not have faith enough and power enough to grapple with this enemy from hell. Now do not sit back and say to yourself, "Well, that case is mine. Nobody as yet has had faith for me."

Oft when the heart aweary grows
And sinks 'neath its burdens and care—
Just when the path seems with snares beset,
Then, like refrain of soft-murmured prayer,
Is the clasp of His hand, whole-hearted and free,
The greeting of warmth so tender, so true—
Magnetically drawing hearts closer to Christ,
Restoring lost courage, faith to renew.

My friend, that is the hand of Jesus. He has already prayed for you; He has already purchased it for you. You are not alone when you have Jesus.

Chapter 20

Broken Back Healed

*T*he good Book declares that we overcome by the blood of the Lamb and the word of our testimony. Because I know that the Lord will bless to your heart another account of a modern miracle, I want to draw your attention to a healing that rocked Oklahoma City a few years ago. I had rented the Merrie Garden auditorium for a revival campaign not knowing that in the hospital was a poor, broken piece of humanity that everybody thought was destined to be a cripple for the rest of her life. But let me take you to the fair grounds in that same city about a month before I started my meeting.

The crowd gasped for breath!

Two thousand feet in the air the great silvery plane was circling around and around. With heads bent back and eyes anxious, the throngs of people on the fair grounds looked at the daredevil woman who was climbing out on the wings of the plane. Crawling along while the plane continued to fly, she at last reached the very tip of the wing and while the crowd waited breathless below, she hesitated for a moment before she made the jump.

The woman was Mrs. Zeva Parker of Oklahoma City, known throughout the length and breadth of the land as "Dare-Devil French

Bobby." She had traveled through many states doing daredevil stunts and had issued a challenge to the whole world for flag pole sitting and other feats of daring. She had [been] suspended hour after hour by a pulley one hundred feet above the throngs on the sidewalk below, and many and varied had been her feats of daring.

The crowd in the Oklahoma City Fair Grounds watched breathlessly as she prepared to make the leap. Clinging for a moment to the edge of the great silver bird, she at last hurled herself into space. As she started down at break-neck speed, she pulled the strings of the parachute that was fastened to her back.

Then a tragedy—the 'chute failed to open to its full resistance, and tearing through the air came the body of the girl daredevil. She fell 2000 feet in 80 seconds. Two thousand feet, falling, to what seemed was sure death, and no time to pray!

Amidst the shrieks of the people, she crumpled to earth and lay prone upon the ground. The ambulance siren sounded, and quickly she was borne away to the hospital. The examination showed that the back was broken in three places, and seven ribs were fractured.

Suffering anguish and pain, she was placed in a plaster of paris cast and the weary days came and went. Forty-five days had come and gone when the happiest day of her life was to dawn.

The revival meetings had started in Merrie Garden and the suffering girl had heard that the Lord was healing the sick. She had known Him as a Savior once, but the call of the world had been too strong and she had gone back to the wages of sin. On her bed of pain, she had nothing to do but think. She had been so near death; so very near, that the door seemed open. She knew she was not ready to die, and the thought brought anguish to her heart. The result was that the ambulance of the Watts & McAtee Funeral Parlors backed up to the door and "Dare-Devil French Bobby" was placed on the bed and carried to the meetings.

It was Tuesday night, and the sick were to be prayed for. She requested prayer. I went to the bedside of the suffering girl and said, "Do you want me to look to the Lord in prayer for you?" Her eyes filled with tears. "No," she said. "No, not yet, I dare not ask Him to touch my body until He has first touched my soul." In a moment she was crying out to God, and the blessed Man of Galilee came and touched her, and she found peace in the salvation of her Lord.

The following night she was brought back to the meetings, and after the services were over, a little group of people gathered around her for prayer. Were they hoping against hope? Were they praying in vain? Had not the doctor said that she could not ever bend her back again and that it would be months or perhaps a year before she could ever walk? Still they prayed, and suddenly, Zeva Parker became dead to this world—lost in the Spirit of God. Her heart filled with the joy of His divine presence. She reached out and touched Him. The miracle happened!

In an instant, in the twinkling of an eye, she was healed.

She jumped to her feet, and while the shouts of praise rang through the building, she walked up and down, both arms in the air, crying and praising God.

What a victory!

Her body was still encased in a plaster of paris cast, but in spite of its tremendous weight she walked out of the building and was taken home.

When the morning dawned, the sun was smiling on the happiest home in Oklahoma City. The cast was off, and the girl with the broken back was running around to the neighbors, telling the story of the healing power of Jesus Christ. When one of the neighbor's children, eyes wide open with amazement, asked the little son of "Dare-Devil French Bobby" who healed his mother, he replied, "No doctor made my mama well; it was just Jesus."

Is it any wonder that her life has been dedicated to God?

Zeva Parker is just another living example of the great truth that Jesus Christ is the same, yesterday and today and forever.

When we come in living contact with miracles of God's power like the one I have just described, does it not inspire you to renewed faith as you look up into the eyes of our blessed Savior? Remember that one healing, just one, is proof that healing is for today.

The divine healing that we preach is not power of mind over matter, nor is it psychological; it comes only through faith in the person and power of a living Jesus. The same Christ who walked through the narrow twisting lanes of old Jerusalem walks through the corridors of the hospital or by your sick bed this day.

Chapter 21

Miracle in Yakima

Paralyzed Girl Healed in Answer to Prayer

*L*et me now give you the story of a little girl, written by a minister of the gospel who attended the meeting. Her name: Erma Wilkinson; her address: Wenatchee, Washington. The minister's story follows.

"The great throng that had filled the tabernacle was streaming out through the doors, the shuffle of thousands of feet upon the sidewalk, the shout of friend greeting friend, the humming of some favorite gospel chorus all mingled with the strident blare of horns as hundreds of automobiles wheeled into line and sped away, each with its cargo of passengers made happy by what their ears had heard and their eyes had seen of the glory and the power of the Lord.

"For it had been healing night at the Price revival, and once more the Lord had graciously confirmed the Word with signs following. The entire service, from beginning to end, had been one of those soul-lifting, faith-inspiring seasons that one so often feels the need of and hungers for.

"The vast audience sat transfixed, as with eager ears and receptive hearts they drank in the Spirit-indicted message. As Dr. Price, perceptibly moved by the power of the Holy Ghost, moved on into his sermon, one could not help but remember the words spoken [about] the Master, that 'He spake not as the scribes, but as one having authority.'

"'Have faith in God,' the evangelist pleaded, and lifting high his right hand, shouted, 'The Christ of Galilee in the long ago is the Christ of Yakima today.'

"The appeal went home. The Spirit had done His work in many hearts. For not only had the Christ of the cross been speaking through His servant, but walking through the aisles and among the pews as well.

"The climax was reached, the sermon ended. God seemed everywhere! The speaker was saying, 'Friends, I leave it with you. I shall not urge.' Through a half suppressed sob I heard him saying, 'How many in this great audience tonight need Jesus?' Hands, hands, hands were lifted everywhere. 'Come sister, come on brother,' pleaded the evangelist. Soon the aisles were crowded with people coming. The long altars were crowded. The front row of seats was cleared and as quickly filled with seekers.

"What a picture! What a sight to behold! Men, women, boys and girls, the lame and the stalwart, all kneeling, praying, consecrating, and accepting Jesus as their Savior. What a petition ascended to Heaven as they all, as with one voice, were laying their burdens at the feet of Him who said, 'And I, if I be lifted up from the earth, will draw all men unto Me.' Dr. Price led while all followed in a prayer of unison. A wave of victory swept along the altars as seekers rejoiced in the God of their salvation.

"It was time to pray for the sick, and Miss Carvel was arranging the healing lines upon the great platform. The choir began to sing 'What a Friend We Have in Jesus' and was joined by the orchestra and audience. Once more the heavenly choir seemed to have come back to earth to sing of Him whose birth they had heralded to the shepherds on the far-away hills of Judea. Every doubt and fear seemed to be swept away on the mighty billows of song. Faith and assurance seemed to pervade the heart of each one waiting to be prayed for.

A Healing Meeting

"It was a great moment, with thousands of eager and expectant eyes looking on, when Dr. Price, all a-tremble under the presence of God's Spirit, anointed and laid hands on the first lady to be prayed for. With face irradiant with faith, with her hands lifted toward heaven and her heart aflame of His promise, the power of God surged through her body and she went down under the power—lost in the presence and glory of Him by whose 'stripes' she was healed.

"A wave of victory swept over the great audience and across the platform. Saints wept for joy as together we sang 'In His arms He'll take and fold thee, thou shalt find a solace there.' God was moving in Yakima. Nearly every one prayed for went down under the power and many, many were healed by power divine.

"All adults having been prayed for, the audience was dismissed and swiftly leaving the tabernacle, when Miss Carvel called Dr. Price to pray for an invalid little girl who had been carried to the platform by her mother and friends. She was a hopeless paralytic, all bent and drawn by infantile paralysis [commonly referred to as polio—*Editor*]. A sweet faced little girl of ten years with streaming golden curls playing idly about her face, now pale and wan as the result of her months of intense suffering.

"When prayed for, her weakened, tender body seemed to swoon and tremble under the power of God. Presently her left hand, all drawn and closed by the dread malady, was seen to come open. God was working. Suddenly she swung her left [leg], paralyzed for months, from off the bench, where she was reclining, and stood upon her feet amid the tears and praises of the saints standing by.

"With eyes closed and both hands lifted toward Heaven, her face shone with the glory of her Lord. The [leg] began to move. The knee, stiff for months, began to bend, the ankle and foot, all drawn and crooked, began to receive strength and straightened out. Oh! What a moment it was! A divine presence was felt by all. The child, now lost in the presence and glory of Him who said, 'Suffer the little children to come unto Me, and forbid them not,' began to walk across the platform, seemingly oblivious of her surroundings, and for probably one hour continued to walk across the platform and up and down the steps.

"She was completely healed. Added strength came to her body with every step she took. Joy and praise were unbounded and the crowd was loath to leave the place where the stately steppings of the Man of Galilee had been so evident."

This is one of the outstanding miracles of modern times, and a sight never to be forgotten by those present.

The Mother's Story

Her case in detail, as related by her mother to the writer is: The child was taken ill February 12, and had 16 or more convulsions from 10:00 that evening to 4:00 the next morning. She was treated by doctors at home and later removed to the hospital. She was in the Deaconess Hospital, Wenatchee, Washington, where her parents reside, for seven weeks under the care of Dr. Leedy. She was also examined by Drs. Kimes and Garinger while in the hospital.

The left [leg] was paralyzed so there was no feeling when pricked by a pin. The leg was badly twisted, as was also the ankle and foot, the toes being drawn under. Her left knee was stiff, rendering the [leg] perfectly rigid, the left arm rendered partially useless and the left hand was drawn shut.

Her stomach and bowels were partially paralyzed, rendering it extremely difficult for any food to be taken. Her eyesight was seriously affected and dimmed. Her hearing was affected and dulled.

After returning home from the hospital, where medical treatment failed to produce any results, and immediately before she was taken to Yakima to be prayed for, she was taken by the parents to the office of Provost, where X-ray photographs were taken of her stomach and bowels. The stomach showed that it was drawn out of shape, the opening into the intestine drawn nearly closed.

Her left limb was placed in two casts, the first one being broken by the severe drawing of the ankle. The parents, despairing of hope, ordered a wheel chair from Montgomery Ward, which arrived on Saturday before the mother received a letter the following Monday telling her of the Price revival campaign in Yakima, asking her to bring the child to the meeting to be prayed for.

The mother brought the girl to Yakima and carried her into the tabernacle every day to meeting for seven days before she was prayed for on July 3, as recorded in the testimony above, when she was completely healed.

As the writer is taking this testimony from the girl and her mother, Erma is sitting before him with her shoes on, legs crossed and laughing and enjoying the situation. All soreness is gone from her [legs] and her natural strength restored.

Well, praise God. The Fourth of July was a great day for America, but July the third was celebrated in two worlds as the praises of the blood-washed of earth and the angels of Heaven resounded to the glory of Him to whom triumph belongs.

This then is the story of the minister who held the little cripple on his knee and who witnessed the mighty healing power of God. Sufferer, whoever and wherever you are, look away now to the great physician, Jesus of Nazareth, through whose stripes you too can be healed.

Chapter 22

Healing for Today

I want to deal now with the question of the healing Christ for the days in which we live. It is generally admitted, even by the opponents of divine healing, that in the days when the Master was here on earth, the miracles attributed to Him actually took place. The lame walked, the blind saw, and the deaf heard. The poor had the gospel preached unto them. There are scores of people who maintain that those things were only for the days of Jesus and the early Christian Church. They declare emphatically that we are in error when we attempt to usurp a ministry for this period that God never intended for this time. What are the scriptural facts in the case? Is there a biblical answer to such criticism?

As a preacher of the gospel of the Lord Jesus Christ, I confess that I could never face a congregation again if I did not believe that Jesus is the same yesterday, today, and forever.

I look down from behind the sacred desk at congregations both large and small. What emotions surge within those breasts? Some are warm and receptive. Others are cold and critical. Some are bitter because they resent the treatment the world has given them. Others are broken and their hearts are tender before God. Some are sick, blind, feeble—filled with pain and suffering. Others who look robust and well perhaps are carrying about with them a tragedy that the world knows nothing about. As I look into their faces, there is one thought that adds wings to my words and puts assurance in my voice. I know that my Jesus is able to meet every need. By every need I mean just what I say—every need. That covers both soul and body. "My God shall supply all your need," declared the apostle in the days of the long ago. Then he went on to tell us how it could be done. How could I preach if, looking into the faces of those poor people, I believed in my heart that there were *some* needs that God could *not* meet—that there would be *some* from whom the Lord would turn aside. I could not preach with assurance. I could not cry, "Come to Jesus," while in the background of my mind there would lurk the thought that only some might come and be satisfied, while the rest would discover that Jesus has a different ministry today than He had in the days of the long ago.

If the critics of divine healing get down on their knees before God and turn over the pages of the sacred Word, they will search the Bible in vain for scriptural proof of their position. In the great commission, the Lord told his disciples that they were to go out into all the world and preach the gospel to every creature—every *creature*. Thank God for that. In the all-inclusive gospel that they were to present, there was salvation for the soul, and healing for the body. There were certain signs that were to follow them that believe. There was the promise that they should lay hands on the sick and they should recover. Yes, thank God, healing is for today.

The Acts of the Holy Ghost

I want to remind you also, that what the translators have called the Acts of the Apostles should really be termed the "Acts of the Holy Ghost." There is not the slightest doubt in my mind but what Jesus Himself healed by the power of the Holy Ghost. We have no record that He preached a sermon until He was anointed to do so by the Holy Ghost.

After He was baptized in the Jordan, He went into the synagogue in the town where He spent His boyhood days. Mounting the pulpit steps, He declared, "The *Spirit of the Lord is* upon me for He has anointed me to preach." When Jesus healed the man by the pool that had five porches, when He stirred the whole city of Capernaum by the miracles of healing that He wrought, we must remember that the day of Pentecost had not yet come. It was not yet the dispensation of the Holy Spirit. Jesus had not yet atoned for sin by His death on Calvary's cross, *yet He forgave sins.* He spoke pardon and peace to troubled hearts and men were born again through His redeeming love. Is it possible that the Holy Spirit would heal *before* the dawning of the day of His dispensation and then refuse to do it in these days which the Bible calls the dispensation of the Holy Ghost?

The same Spirit that fell upon Jesus, as in bodily form of a dove, fell upon the disciples as they gathered in the upper room on the day of Pentecost. That marked the beginning of His dispensation. The Acts of the Apostles record that the same Holy Ghost displayed the *same* healing power in the lives and ministry of the disciples *after* Pentecost as displayed in the life of Jesus *before* Pentecost.

The disciples themselves had no healing power, apart and separate from the Holy Ghost. They had no power to perform miracles. If the power had been given to them apart from the presence of the Holy Spirit when they died, the gifts would have died with them. They, however, were careful to preach the same gospel that had been committed unto them. As they passed on to their reward, the same Holy Spirit with exactly the *same* ministry—and the *same* power to heal—came into the hearts of regenerate men. Now if healing is not for this day, then one of two things must have happened. Either the Holy Ghost, the *one who really brings healing,* is not in our midst, or He does not have the same ministry in the closing days of the dispensation as He did in the opening days!

We get our healing, of course, through the atoning work of Jesus on Calvary. We shall have something to say about that later. It is the Holy Spirit, however, who takes the things that have been purchased and made possible through the atoning work of Christ, and acting as the administrator of the Godhead, delivers these priceless gifts to the waiting hearts of men. His ministry is to execute for us the blessings that were purchased by the redemptive work of Christ, and presented to all of mankind in the seven redemptive names of our Lord.

The Seven Redemptive Names

When we unlock the treasure chest of typical truth we find those seven diamonds of divine love shining and sparkling against the dark background of Old Testament days.

Here they are in all of their luster and beauty.

- *Jehovah-Shammah*—The Lord is there (present).

- *Jehovah-Shalom*—The Lord our Peace.

- *Jehovah-Ra-ah*—The Lord is my Shepherd.

- *Jehovah-Jireh*—The Lord will provide.

- *Jehovah-Nissi*—The Lord is our banner—victor or captain.

- *Jehovah-Tsidkenu*—The Lord our Righteousness.

- *Jehovah-Rapha*—I am the Lord thy Physician, or I am the Lord that healeth thee.

What right have we, what authority has any man to repudiate the redemptive name of Jehovah-Rapha, while acknowledging the other six names are still the redemptive names of our Christ? I maintain that if one can with impunity declare that the Lord in these days is not the one who heals us, then anyone else would have a right to throw out the other redemptive names of Christ. What I am attempting to do is to burn in your heart, and do it in such a way that every doubt and fear will flee, that great truth—that divine healing is for today and can become real to *you*. Of course the devil does not want you to be healed! He is the author of sickness. He is the author of disease. He is the one who is responsible for death.

Obedience Through Suffering

Many times ministers have come to me with a story regarding the growth of the Christian life through pain and through suffering. They maintain that we learn obedience by the things we suffer. I admit that there are times when God allows things to come upon us for the purpose of drawing us into a closer relationship with Himself. There are times when He permits things to happen to our lives—yes, even in our physical bodies—in order that He might work out in us His own purposes and will. The Bible very clearly states that the Lord chastens those whom He loves. He does it for a purpose. But I ask you, does He continue to chasten *after the purpose has been accomplished?* If it is true that we learn obedience by the things which we suffer, does He make us continue in our suffering *after* we have learned obedience? If your little girl at home has been naughty and you chastise her in order that through the chastisement she might learn the lesson, do you spend the rest of your life doing nothing else but whip her?

The answer to that question is obvious. When the chastisement has fulfilled its purpose, *it ceases.* It is not your will that your child should be chastised. Your will is that she should become a better girl. It is not God's will that His people should suffer. His will is that we should be led into green pastures and made to lie down by still waters. But if the road to green pastures is one that is rough and steep, certainly the Lord would never want us to lie down in the midst of a thorny road and say that it is His will that we stay there the rest of our lives.

The fact of the matter is that people who have not faith for healing, because they will not believe God, try to find an excuse in order to substantiate their position. In order to do that, they run over a thousand promises in the Word. They distort the clear teaching of the Gospels and the Epistles when they take out of its setting some obscure text, hang their hats and coats on it, and sit underneath with a mournful expression, asserting that they are in God's will.

I cannot for the life of me understand how a perfectly healthy preacher can walk into a room where a little woman is suffering with cancer, and declare unto her that it might be God's *will for her to suffer* that excruciating agony and awful pain. I like to go into that sick room having read my Bible and with the bells of the promises of God ringing in my heart. I like to go in there feeling my feet are on the solid Rock of Ages. I like to hold my Bible high in the air and plead the blood of Jesus and rebuke the devil and proclaim the gospel that Jesus Christ is the same yesterday, today, and forever. I declare unto you that by the name of Jesus and by the power of the Holy Spirit, disease has fled and the Lord has taken all the pain out of that body until the renewed heart shouts for joy.

Why Seek Health?

Again let me remind you that if it is God's will that His children should be sick and suffer, we have no right to telephone the doctor to come and give us medicine in order that the will of the Lord might be broken. If it is God's will for you to be sick, then it is a sin for you to pray to be well. It means that every physician in the country is attempting to frustrate the purposes of God. It necessarily follows that every trained nurse is trampling under feet the will of God. It means that you yourself should not pray to get well, because by so doing, it would be violating the will of God. The only logical and scriptural thing for people to do who maintain that position, is to sit down like Elijah under the Juniper tree of their troubles, and just pray God to take their lives that they might be happy in the by-and-by.

It Makes a Difference

Some years ago I was conducting a healing meeting in a town in the Midwest. As is the case wherever I go, the pastors of the city were divided regarding the ministry of healing. It was a bitter disappointment to me when a man for whom I had a profound respect, and who ordinarily was kind and tender in his ministry, came out with a scathing denunciation of the work the Lord had called me to do. He declared most emphatically that healing was not for today. He said we were wrecking the faith of the people and destroying the confidence that men and women had in God. He declared that we should preach Christ for the soul, but not for the body. From his pulpit he told of the lives of people who had become illustrious through their suffering. His ministry undoubtedly had an effect upon the town, and it was hard for me to pray for the sick against the atmosphere of unbelief. Do not forget that unbelief sometimes tied the hands of Jesus.

Toward the end of the campaign, as I was leaving the building one night, I was amazed to see that preacher waiting at the door. I could see that he was under the stress of some tremendous emotion. His big frame shook under the throb of his voice. It appeared that his own little girl was sick. Not only that, she was at the very gate of death. She was only 12 years of age, a beautiful, tender, sweet little flower that God had given him to love and to cherish. An ordinary cold had developed into pneumonia that was followed by double pneumonia. The doctors had practically given up hope. He wanted me to go into his house and pray.

As we rode together in the car towards the home, I said to him, "Doctor, what did you do when your little girl fell sick?" He looked at me with tears in his eyes—this man who did not believe in divine healing. "Why, I went to my room and prayed, of course." I wanted to say, "Well, my brother, if it is right for you to pray for your own little girl, why should you object to my praying for somebody else's little girl?" I did not, however. It would have been cruel for me to upbraid him at such a time as that. You see, my friends, he instinctively went to his knees. You say it was the natural thing for him to do. He needed God and he just cried out for God.

I went with him into a big room and anointed and prayed for the girl. She opened her eyes and smiled and I know it was not my fancy when I declared, "I feel the fever leaving her." She did not get up and run around as I had prayed she would. She rather settled back with the words, "I believe Jesus" on her lips and rested patiently in the Lord. From that moment she recovered. In a few days she was out again. Her father rejoiced in the healing Christ. One day as we walked together down the street that good preacher turned to me and said, "Price, it is easy to preach about the ministry of suffering when the suffering is in the other fellow's home. I believe it was the Holy Spirit that drove me to my knees, and then sent me out after a man who had faith enough to believe. What a wonderful, wonderful Savior!"

He Is Able

I do not know into whose hands this volume will fall. Someone may be reading it in distant China—or it may be read by some missionary to a dark skinned congregation in the heart of Africa. It may be that some poor sufferer, propped up on a hospital bed in the homeland, will be scanning these pages. One thing I know, my wonderful, wonderful Lord is able *to supply all of your needs* according to His riches in glory. The Holy Spirit is by your side to take the things of Christ and make them plain unto you. Fasten your eyes upon the One who came to redeem you. Look into His blessed face and call Him Jehovah-Rapha. You will hear His sweet and tender voice whispering to your heart, "I am the Lord that healeth thee."

Chapter 23

Six Steps to Healing

o you who are in need of the healing touch of Jesus, I want in all humility to make a few suggestions. I am not going to be dogmatic. There are no hard and fast rules that we must follow. However, during the years in which I have been praying for the sick, I have observed certain things. Those observations have led me to certain conclusions. I am absolutely persuaded that these conclusions are scriptural. There are a few steps up which people have come from their condition of sickness to the possession of divine healing.

When we give our bodies to the Lord we can take the Lord for our body. We are instructed to bring not only our heart, but also our *bodies* to the Lord, and are told that it is but our reasonable service. The Bible declares that such a surrender and consecration is acceptable unto the Lord Himself. It seems to me that we can look at this divine healing question with the eyes of faith when we recognize that He to whom we have given our hearts has received them, and healed them of their sin. Why should we not then believe that He to whom we give our bodies can also heal them of their physical infirmities and pains? We could then, of a truth, say that our healing would be for His glory. Let me give you the steps up which so many have traveled to ultimate victory in the name of the Lord Jesus Christ.

The First Step

Get hold of a promise and stand on it. Recognize that it is for you. Don't try to cover the whole world with that promise, but tell the Lord that in His infinite mercy and love He has condescended to give that promise to you. It is your priceless possession. When you realize it, you will treasure it in your heart more than you have ever treasured any jewel in your life. You will hold it so close to you that you will never want to let it go. You will declare, "It is mine—mine—mine."

The Second Step

Bring your burden, your problem, your need, to the Lord and leave it there. Refuse to worry about it. Whether or not there is any manifestation of divine healing power, hold the Lord to His promise and tell Him that you have laid your burden at His nail-pierced feet. He is the Burden Bearer. The chastisement of our peace was upon Him. He assumed our sins. That is the reason why we do not have to carry them any more. He died our death and gave us His life. He bore our sickness and carried our sorrows. Because of the greatness of His heart and love, He invites us to come with our burdens and leave them at His feet.

So many times we bring our burdens to the Lord, intercede about them, supplicate about them, and then promptly take them away with us, only to bring them back with us the following night. To do so is totally unscriptural and shows a lack of faith in God. Bring your burdens and lay them at His nail-pierced feet and say, "Dear Lord Jesus, though all the world be false, Your promises are sure. Forgive me for my worry, for my fretting, for my unbelief. I lay my burdens before You. In Your Word You have said that You care for me."

When we see the lilies spinning in distress,
Taking thought to manufacture loveliness;
When we see the birds all building barns for store,
'Twill be time for us to worry—not before.

The Third Step

Put your trust in the Lord. Do not put your trust in feeling or in manifestation or in any physical demonstration. Worry looks at self but faith looks to God. Fretting looks down to the earth and beholds its cold-ness and its meanness. Trust looks at the skies and sees the star of hope, the morning star of the promise that heralds the coming of the Sun of Righteousness. When we put our trust in the Lord, we shall discover that our worry will have gone. Do not think of self, but keep your eyes fast on Jesus. "Trust in the Lord with all thine heart; and lean not unto thine own understanding. In all thy ways acknowledge Him, and He shall direct thy paths."

The Fourth Step

Delight yourself in the Lord. Has it ever occurred to you that you can never delight yourself in the Lord unless you are standing on the promises? You could not come up this fourth step unless you have taken the other three. Delight and worry do not mix. Unless there is trust in the Lord and confidence in His promises, there never could be delight. On the other hand it is almost impossible to climb up the first three steps and not put your foot on the fourth rung of the ladder. Delight is some-thing that comes because doubt is gone.

It is at this point that faith really begins to take hold. Faith believes before it receives and expresses itself in joy. Faith says, "Thank You," on the basis of the fact that the gift has been promised, and gets so happy about it that it commences to praise. Anybody can feel delighted about it after the gift has been received, but it takes real faith to delight oneself in the gift on the basis of the promise. Whenever I come across people who have prayed through until they have touched the Throne, and who are shouting the victory, I see people in whose lives faith is operating in a mighty way.

The Fifth Step

Rest in the Lord. Wait patiently for Him. Intercession has its place, but there must come a time when intercession ceases and praise com-mences. Supplication will reach the ears of God, but the answer comes on the wings of faith and trust. There might not be very much faith in the prayer, "Give me, Lord," but there certainly has to be faith when you say, "Thank you, Lord." Oh, that the saints of God would learn the lesson of resting in the Lord and waiting, even if we have to wait patiently—patiently—for Him. We have His blessed Word to assure us that He will give us the desires of our heart.

"There is a secret place of rest,
God's saints alone may know;
Thou shalt not find it east nor west,
Though seeking to and fro;
A cell where Jesus is the door,
His love the only key;
Who enter will go out no more,
But there with Jesus be."

The Sixth Step

Give God the glory. Don't compare your faith with the faith of others. Do not become spiritually proud. Do not allow self satisfaction to exalt you in your own esteem more than what you really are. Our blessed Master is the author of every good and perfect gift. To Him we owe our everything. To Him belong our praise and our adoration. To Him alone we bow the knee in reverence and worship. God has condescended to talk with man. Divinity has breathed upon humanity. The jewelry of Heaven has been given to the poor undeserving creatures of earth. Always give God the glory and then God will give you His smile.

Chapter 24

Healing and Atonement

I have previously stated that healing was purchased for us by the atoning ministry of the Lord Jesus Christ. As I have gone up and down the country preaching the gospel of Christ for the body as well as for the soul, quite a number of ministers have criticized my work. Many of them seem to believe that Christ can and does heal the sick today, but they strenuously object to my preaching healing in the atonement.

Not so very long ago I received a letter from one very well known minister who stated that if I were to leave the question of healing being in or out of the atonement entirely alone, and merely pray for the sick, I would find a more hearty cooperation wherever I went. He went on to declare that it would not matter. But it does matter. If healing is not in the atonement, then we come to the Lord beseeching him out of His mercy to work a miracle in our lives. We do not come claiming healing as our inheritance. We can ask for it, but we cannot appropriate it. If healing is in the atonement, the working of the miracle in our physical bodies is not so much a question of supplication as it is of appropriation. If it is not in the atonement, it has not been purchased; but if it is in the atonement we can come with boldness, knowing that our Lord has paid for our sickness and carried our sorrows.

I would like to remind you that divine healing through the atoning work of Jesus was very clearly taught in every one of the Old Testament types. The 14th and 15th chapters of Leviticus prove conclusively that it was only through the atonement that healing was brought about. The priest had to make atonement for the healing of the leper before that man could be delivered by the manifestation of the power of God. In the 16th chapter of Numbers, we read that 14,700 people had died of the plague. Aaron, clothed in his priestly garments and standing in the dignity of his mediatorial office, made atonement in order that the plague might be lifted. He was very clearly typifying that matchless One who should come after him. As we travel down the glorious corridors of the Old Testament story, type after type declares the fact of atonement, not only for sin, but for deliverance from disease as well.

Beloved in the Lord, Christ has purchased your salvation. He has also paid for the healing of your body. Do not let the devil bluff you out of what is yours—yours—yours, because of God's great compassion and love. It cost your blessed Savior something to bring to the door of your heart His own healing power. Look up through the clouds and shout the victory. Faith will pull down the Jericho walls of unbelief. Every obstacle can be overcome and the glory of the Lord made manifest in your body.

Many devout and well known leaders in the Christian faith have declared without hesitation that healing was and is a part of the atoning ministry of Jesus. Dr. R.E. Stanton, a former moderator of the General Assembly of the Presbyterian Church, has declared, "It is my aim to show that the atonement of Christ lays the foundation equally for deliverance from sin and for deliverance from disease; that complete provision has been made for both; that in the exercise of faith under the conditions prescribed, we have the same reason to believe that the body may be delivered from sickness that we have that the soul shall be delivered from sin; in short, that both branches of the deliverance stand on the same ground, and that it is necessary to include both in any true conception of what the gospel offers to mankind."

Bishop Reese, of the Episcopal Church, as a representative of a commission of physical healing, appointed by his church, submitted the following report: "The healing of the body is an essential element of the gospel, and must be preached and practiced....God wills our health, that the Church, the Body of Christ has the same commission and the same power as The Head, that we churchmen, with this true conception of God as Creative Love, must now give a sinning and suffering world this full Gospel of salvation from sin and its inevitable consequences."

Bishop Charles H. Brent, who was head of all chaplains in France when the boys were overseas affirms: "He who waves away the healing power of Christ as belonging only to the New Testament times is not preaching the whole Gospel. God was, and is, the Savior of the body as well as the soul."

So we could continue with quotations from Dr. A.B. Simpson, Andrew Murray, A.T. Pierson, and others. All of these men are shining lights and are known the world around as able expositors of the Bible. They declare without hesitation that healing is a part of the atoning work of Jesus.

But what is best of all is the fact that results prove it. I do not want to be cynical when I make the following statement, but I do want to call your attention to one very evident fact. The ministers who are getting tangible results in the healing of the body are almost always the ones who believe in healing in the atonement. Why is it that during the years, thousands of people have come to our services from every denomination in the country—both Catholic and Protestant—and have requested us to bring their case before the throne of grace?

Chapter 25

Hindrances to Appropriating Faith

he purpose of this book, dear reader, is to bring to your attention the glorious opportunity that is yours of coming in vital contact with the healing Christ. We must admit that it is sometimes easier to talk about faith than it is to exercise it. There are certain spiritual realities about which we are thoroughly convinced—yet it seems to be very difficult to interpret them in terms of practical experience. More than one sick person has said to me, "I believe it alright, but then it is so difficult for me to appropriate the thing I believe."

Belief is the doorway through which we pass into the beautiful garden of appropriating faith. We have been looking through the glass at the flowers of the promises that grow in the garden of the Lord. We knew that they are there—we could see them—we believe them—but the glass hindered us from reaching out our hands and touching them. There are thousands of men who believe in salvation but have never experienced it. There are also thousands who believe in divine healing but have never received it. There can come a time, however, when the door of grace divine will swing open and we step across the threshold into the midst of the garden of the Lord. Perhaps you are in that position. Perhaps you believe—but you are finding it so very, very difficult to receive. Allow me in humility to tell you of a few things that I have found have been hindrances to appropriating faith.

Self-Pity

First: There is self-pity. We know that it is not a pleasant thing to be sick. When you are in pain, it is perfectly natural that you should be sorry because you are in physical agony. Other people are sorry for you too. I have discovered, however, that this pity can be carried to such an extent that it is put up as a barricade against the healing power of the Lord Jesus.

Some time ago I was called to the bedside of a poor woman who had been incapacitated for a number of years. The family was very, very poor. The children were doing their best to keep the home in order, but little tots cannot be expected to do the work as well as mother when she is well and strong. The good husband had to go out day by day to earn his bread by the sweat of his brow. It was impossible for him to do very much of the housework. The good sister who was suffering on her bed of sickness had become irritated, nervous, and filled with self-pity because of her own condition as well as the state of her home.

I went to talk with her, but instead she talked to me. For over one hour she poured into my ears her tale of sorrow. When I could see that she was determined to continue along this line I stopped her and said, "Now sister, you have talked for over one hour about yourself—let me talk for a little while about Jesus."

You see, her trouble was that in her self-pity she was looking at herself so much that she did not have time to see Jesus. When she started to tell me about her troubles I insisted that she tell me something about her blessings. She told me that she did not have very many. I pointed out to her that there were a thousand ways in which her condition could be worse.

"When upon Life's billows you are tempest tossed,
When you are discouraged, thinking all is lost,
Count your many blessings, name them one by one,
And it will surprise you what the Lord hath done."

In a little while the atmosphere of that home commenced to change. Her eyes took on a different light as I continued to talk about Jesus. Then one of the workers who had come with me to the sick bed very softly sang:

"Oh, touch the hem of His garment
And thou too shall be free.
His healing power, this very hour
Will bring new life to thee."

When the husband came home at the close of his working day he was greeted at the door by his good wife. She was still weak from the effects of her long stay in bed—but she had touched the Lord and she had found deliverance in the healing Christ. Sometime later she said to me, "Whenever things come to me now in life that would make me rebellious, critical, or fault finding I always begin to sing 'Count your blessings,' and it is not long before the clouds have rolled away."

Self-pity looks at self, but faith looks away to Jesus. Elijah and his servant could be in the same tent and yet see two different things. The heart of one could be filled with victory while the other was filled with dismay.

Fear Is an Enemy

Second: Fear is a great hindrance. God's Word tells us that perfect love casteth out fear. Perfect love means perfect trust. You tell me that you love Jesus, then I answer you, "You ought to trust Him."

You tell me that you do trust Him, and yet you are sick. If that be the case, just keep on trusting and hold this great truth in your heart. He loves you—the very hairs of your head are all numbered. He has promised never to leave you and His Word of truth and power declares that all things are working together for your good. You see, my friend, when your heart is filled with fear you do not follow your Guide in the way that you should.

Some time ago I made a trip through some caverns beautiful beyond my power of description to describe and yet, had I been alone, they would have meant death. Hundreds and hundreds of feet below the surface of the ground and along their gigantic halls for mile after mile, I walked the narrow ledge pathways in company with my guide. He knew the way. Without him I would have been lost. I was not afraid because I put my trust in him. Life is something like that. When you put your trust in Jesus you should never be afraid. God has not forsaken you—He has not abandoned you—He has not left you to grope your way through the darkness along the paths of suffering and sorrow. You will understand the purpose of it by-and-by. Do not let the devil discourage you, but just raise your eyes heavenward and say:

> "All the way my Saviour leads me,
> What have I to ask beside?
> Can I doubt His tender mercy
> Who through life has been my guide?
> Heav'nly peace, divinest comfort,
> Here by faith in Him to dwell!
> For I know, whate'er befall me,
> Jesus doeth all things well."

Sing that with your lips, and the nightingale of faith will echo the refrain through the corridors of your soul.

Clouds of Doubt

Third: Another great hindrance to faith is the atmosphere of doubt. Sometimes it is created by unbelievers who surround the sickbed. It is very hard to pray the prayer of faith while some ungodly man stands by with a sneer on his face. Is it not a tragedy when some poor sufferer is endeavoring to reach out his hand and touch the hem of His garment, while the members of his own family ridicule and mock? Yet that often happens. Remember that the greater the need, the greater the grace that is given to meet the need. I love to believe that my Lord is sufficient to meet every emergency. He will not hold you responsible for the doubts of others. Do not allow the atmosphere that others may create to mar and spoil the beautiful trust and peace of your own soul. Think what will happen to them when someday you get out of that wheelchair—rise from that bed healed by the power of God! The victory will be all the greater because of the intensity of the battle.

The Song of the Nightingale

Charles Hadden Spurgeon was once leaving his London church when a lady stopped him and said, "Mr. Spurgeon, you said something today that captivated me. You said that faith was the nightingale of the Christian graces. Why did you say that? It seemed so beautiful to me that I thought there must have been a story hidden in your definition."

Mr. Spurgeon said that there was, and then told the following story:

He had been walking down the street of London about a week earlier, when he came across an old friend. The man was exuberant. Patting Mr. Spurgeon on the back, the man said that he had just returned from a week spent at a very rustic farmhouse among the rural beauties of the rolling hills of Devonshire. Every night outside his window a little bird had come to sing in the darkness, a song so beautiful and so sweet that it will live in the memory of the hearer while life itself lasts. It was as if God had wrapped up the song of an angel in a little bundle of feathers and sent it down to earth and called it a nightingale.

Mr. Spurgeon had never heard the nightingale sing. A letter of introduction was hastily written and down to Devonshire went the great London preacher on his quest for the prima donna songstress of nature. When he arrived at the little village the rain was pouring pitilessly down. He trudged along the country lane and then across the field through the old stile by the swaying poplars until he arrived at the farm house door. They were honored at the presence of such an illustrious guest. The preacher was wet and cold. They dried his clothes by the fire, gave him a good supper; and then he went to bed.

No moon was visible in the sky above. Not a star could be seen in the meadows of the heavens. The rain came in torrents and beat upon the slate roof above his head as he tried to sleep. No use to try to stay awake for the nightingale's song on a night like that. But he was mistaken. At midnight—when the storm was at its height—he heard the song that thrilled him to the very depths of his being. Quietly as he could he got out of bed and stole to the window. There in a thorn bush with its breast pressed against a thorn was the nightingale. It was singing as if its heart would break. After the song was over Mr. Spurgeon knelt in prayer. The little bird had preached a sermon to a great preacher that night.

From that time on, faith was called the nightingale of the Christian graces because it could sing in the darkest night when its breast was pressed against a thorn. It could sing in the rain.

So if there is doubt around you—keep singing. If it is raining—keep trusting. To some the rain means nothing but a gloomy day, while to others it means the violets on the hillside in the golden days of spring. Above all, remember that the promises of Jesus are for you. You are His child and He loves you. Trust the Lord. Have faith and confidence in Him and He will give you the desires of your heart.

The Glory of Grace

Fourth: Another great hindrance is the constant dwelling upon the thought that you are not being healed because you are not worthy. You might as well settle it in your mind right now that were you to live ten thousand years you never could be worthy. There never has been a man saved or healed who deserved it. That is where grace comes in. The older I get the more of grace I am putting into my ministry and into my sermons to the sick and suffering and sinful and needy. If we deserved the blessings of God it would not be grace. There is a story—one of my favorites—that I wish to bring to your heart in developing this part of my theme.

Suffer Little Children

Quite a number of years ago I was participating in a great evangelistic campaign in the Midwest. The power of the Lord was present to heal, and many were the miracles of grace divine. I had announced a children's healing service for the following Saturday afternoon, and thousands of people were praying day by day that God would manifest His glory in that service. On Thursday afternoon, two days preceding the healing meeting for children, a little visitor came up on the platform to have a chat. She had a sweet little face completely encircled by golden curls and blue eyes that were beautiful indeed, but they seemed to mirror the sorrow and grief in her little heart. She came to talk to me about the healing service. She was a cripple. From her waist to the soles of her little feet bars of steel encased her poor little body. The tips of her thickly soled shoes barely touched the ground as she hobbled along with the crutches beneath her baby arms. The kind doctors had done everything they could to battle this scourge of infantile paralysis, but as far as they were concerned she was beyond human help.

"When are you going to pray for children, Brother Price?" she asked.

"On Saturday afternoon," was my reply.

Her face took on an expression of ecstasy as she said, "And won't I be happy when I can run and play just like my little friends?"

"Yes, that will be a great day for you, little darling, and I am praying that the good Lord will give us all faith to reach out and touch Him so that your dream might come true. Are you praying every day yourself?"

"Yes, sir," she replied.

"Is your mother praying?" I asked.

She hesitated for a moment and then softly answered, "Yes."

"And is your daddy praying?"

Again there was a noticeable hesitation and she said, "Yes, my daddy is praying too. I must go now...Goodbye."

Away she hobbled as quickly as she could, down the steps, down the aisle, and out of the door of the great auditorium. The following afternoon she came to the meeting a little late, for she could only attend after school. As she came to the platform she burst into tears. Her little body just shook with her sobs as she said to me, "Brother Price, I have come to tell you that I will not be here tomorrow. Jesus...will not . . . heal . . . me."

"What is the trouble?" I asked.

Then she told me the story. She said that she had told a lie and that Jesus had heard her. She had said that her mother and father were both praying. They were not. As a matter of fact she said they had forbidden her to attend the meetings. She said that her father swore at her and that her mother had whipped her for being so foolish as to believe that she could be healed by the power of the Lord. It was not a Christian home—far from it—but the poor little girl had attended the meeting and had heard and believed the story of the healing Christ.

I put my arms around her and did my best to comfort her broken little heart. I told her that Jesus loved her in spite of the fact that she had done wrong and explained to her as best I could the meaning of that word *grace*. It is so big and glorious that even Heaven itself could not contain it. She listened and I dried her weeping eyes with my handkerchief and asked her to kneel with me and pray.

"I cannot kneel, Mr. Price, because of the braces, but I can stand and pray." I told her to sit in my chair and I knelt down by her side, and we prayed together. She left the platform that afternoon with the promise that she would return the following day, and be anointed in the children's healing service and look to the Lord for deliverance. Never shall I forget that Saturday afternoon. She was the third little girl in line. When I prayed nothing happened. That is, nothing that was manifest—nothing that we could see. I prayed the second time and when I opened my eyes she was still standing on her crutches.

Turning to the audience I said, "Everybody pray—please pray...let faith overcome curiosity. Lift your hearts to the Lord in prayer."

A Little Child Shall Lead Them

The whole congregation burst into prayer—many wept and quite a few got on their knees before the Lord. I myself knelt on the platform and cried out my heart to God. When I opened my eyes the little girl was gone! She had climbed down the steps—she was still on her crutches...still as bad as ever she was to all outward appearances. I thought I would encourage her by telling her that all healings were not instant. As in the days of Jesus some began to mend at the hour of prayer.

To my surprise she rebuked me. She did not intend to do so, but she did. Her little eyes flashed with the light of Heaven. She threw back her little curls as she tossed her head and said, "Oh Brother Price, you don't have to talk to me like that. I believe Jesus. Mine is a very hard case, and I don't expect Him to heal me all of a sudden."

Her little voice was vibrant with praise and faith. At the Saturday night service she did not come. All day Sunday I looked for my little girl—but she was not there. Monday afternoon I felt sure that she would make her appearance—but the little girl was not to be found. Thoughts came into my mind of whippings at home—of a swearing father, and of a mother who did not believe. Monday night I looked over the great audience and still my eyes failed to detect her. When the time for the altar call came I invited every man and woman who was unsaved to come and kneel before the Lord, plead the shed blood of Calvary, and give their hearts to Jesus. Then it was I saw my little girl.

Down the long center aisle she came leading by one hand a man and by the other hand a woman. Altar workers rushed to help, but I waved them aside. Right in front of my pulpit they came and I heard her little voice say, "Daddy, you kneel here—and Mother, you kneel here."

I looked at her and then broke into sobs of praise. The crutches were gone—the braces were gone. She walked without a limp. She was healed. That night while the angels in Glory sang the praises of a Redeemer, that father and mother found Christ as Savior. Chorus after chorus rang through the building and for over one hour the people stayed to pray. As I went home that night I could hear a little group of people standing by the auditorium door singing "Jesus breaks every fetter and He sets me free."

The healing had occurred just as they were sitting down to the evening meal. That little girl had bowed her head to pray and the glory of the Lord had rested upon her. My friend, will you not learn this lesson? It is not because we are worthy—not because we deserve it—but because of the infinite love of God that such marvelous grace has been bestowed upon us.

Never Give Up

Fifth: Another great and tremendous hindrance is discouragement.

"Never be sad or despondent,
When you have faith to believe
Look on the side that is brightest,
Trust in the Lord, and receive.

Never give up, never give up
Never give up to your sorrows,
Jesus will bid them depart,
Sing when your troubles are greatest,
Trust in the Lord and take heart."

As I have contacted the sick I presume that we have had more "discouragement" to fight with than any other hindrance that impedes the heart as it travels along the highway of faith. If Jesus was not alive then we would have every cause for discouragement. I think that one of the most discouraged families I ever met was in Edmonton, Alberta. Today I know of no happier group of people. I count them among my dearest friends.

Then they were living in the darkness of despair—so desperate their plight that a loving father told me that he would not have cared if the bridge had opened up and the cold waters of the river beneath could have put an end to their sorrows. Today they are an evangelistic party on fire for God, and have been mightily used of the Lord in bringing salvation and healing to hundreds of needy people all over this American continent.

I refer to the Fox Evangelistic Party. They stand out as living examples of the power of Jesus to heal in the days in which we live. When some doubting preacher tells me that he does not believe in "miracles," I refer him to these living witnesses, testimonies so glorious that they alone repudiate the argument of every critic of divine healing in the land.

Chapter 26

From the Gates of Death

A Modern Miracle

(Miss E.M. Fox, Naselle, Washington)

I want to give you these testimonies and I think it would be better if they could be given in the words of the two people themselves. Imagine yourself in a meeting. Miss Ethel Fox of Naselle, Washington, evangelist of the cross, stands up to testify. These are her words:

"First of all I wish to say that every word of this testimony is written for the glory and honor of my Lord who hath wrought this marvelous miracle in my life. Praise His name! I know that God lives; that His Son, Jesus, bore the sin and sickness of all this world. I know because the Bible, God's Word, declares it, and I know because He not only saved me, but healed my body when all earthly hope was gone. So in praise unto Him, and with the prayer in my heart that some other weary sufferer may find peace and healing for soul and body, in His name, I give this account of my suffering and healing.

"I was born with every organ in my body out of place. My heart, as well as being out of place, was too small, and in later years, owing to chronic rheumatism, became diseased. An operation was performed to put the stomach and intestines back in their proper places, but was utterly unsuccessful. Kindhearted doctors did all in their power to relieve my sufferings, but to no avail.

"I had an operation for appendicitis and afterwards adhesions developed, for which I had another operation, but in a few months adhesions formed again. Then in 1918 I had attacks of influenza and pleurisy. My lungs were affected and then began the long, tedious "cure" for tuberculosis. My throat was also tubercular. I lay in bed in a tent for several months, when the physician pronounced me sufficiently improved to allow of my being up a part of the day.

"Just at this time I lost my dear mother—God called her home. Shortly after this I had a very serious illness, during which my life was despaired of, but God heard the prayers of my father and spared me. Then it was found necessary to perform another serious operation. The strain proved too much for me; in a short time the tuberculosis was active again. This time I had to go to a sanitorium for treatment. I was there several months and, as I did not improve, but rather grew worse, losing weight continually, I decided to go home, I thought, to die.

"Several years before this I had been confined to my bed for 17 long, weary months with hip joint disease. The disease had become quiescent. Later, an injury to my ankle caused considerable difficulty, and shortly after I left the sanitorium the disease in my leg again became active, and walking became increasingly difficult and painful.

"At a very early age my eyesight failed, and for some years I had to wear colored glasses, for I could not bear the bright light. Doctors said I would eventually become totally blind.

"The operations which I had, were, as I have already stated, quite unsuccessful. I was also afflicted with constipation. Owing to the organs and intestines being out of place, medicine failed to have any effect, and I had to depend almost entirely upon enemas of different kinds, and at times even they would fail, and my whole system would become poisoned. At such times I suffered intensely.

"I have been under the X-ray 20 times, and have had 30 doctors in actual attendance upon me.

"Such was my condition in the year of 1923. I cannot look back upon that weary time without a shudder. Faith began to fail, doubts crept in. 'Why? Why? Why?' was the continual cry of my heart. I saw others going on and making a success of life. Why was I, who so earnestly and ambitiously desired to attain something in the world, stricken down in this way? Doubts crept in upon me, at first almost unawares. I went to church whenever I was able to do so. I did not hear the way of the cross preached as of yore. I would go away with a vague, unnamed dissatisfaction in my heart. I remember once going to church to listen to a previously announced sermon upon the subject of the coming of the Lord. I heard that night that we must not believe the Bible, that we must not expect our blessed Lord to return in the way that His Word says He will; only in a spiritual way will He come, was what I heard.

Faith Clings to the Promise

"When my father and I went home that night, we talked over that which we had heard. My father's faith, praise God, was not shaken, but mine was.

"'Perhaps,' I said, 'he is right and we wrong.' And then, ah, how subtle is the devil. More doubts were whispered to my heart.

"'If,' said the tempter, 'the Bible does not speak the truth regarding this, may there not be many other things not right there?' and I listened to his whisperings. I was a great reader. I read books which increased doubts of the inspired Word of God; books which left me no foundation to stand upon; books which still leave one a God, but deny the deity of the Savior and His power to save; and this, in spite of the fact that God's Word says 'No man cometh unto the Father, but by Me.' Whither was I drifting? I shuddered to think where! From childhood I had always prayed and now with my doubts and fears, to whom should I pray, for what should I pray? But God, whose eye, we read, runs to and fro throughout the whole earth, was watching me and was bringing speedy relief.

"Just at this time, when I was helpless, hopeless and undone, God sent an evangelist to Edmonton, [Alberta], Canada, where I was then living, and also gave me strength to attend a number of the meetings, and I came back to the old, sweet faith in Jesus, and again experienced joy and peace, praise His holy name! A few times in my life, some dear saints of God had spoken to me of healing for the body as well as forgiveness for sins, but I cast the thought from me, saying, 'I suppose God could heal people, but I don't think healing is for these days.' But as the evangelist preached of a Christ who is the same yesterday, today and forever, I began to see that Jesus had a perfect redemption to offer to all who would accept it—a complete redemption from all the curse, praise His holy name! And so one night a number of workers gathered around, anointing me with oil, and prayed the Lord to heal me. I was not healed that night; it was not easy to rid myself of all my old doubts and fears, and I was dull of understanding still, for 'spiritual things are spiritually discerned.' A week after the meetings were concluded, there came to Edmonton that man of God Dr. C.S. Price.

"God increased my strength so that I was sufficiently strong to attend the meetings, which were held in the arena. Never had I been in such meetings before. Never had I been where the Holy Spirit was so honored. The first Tuesday afternoon of the campaign, there was held a service for the sick—a service for the purpose of showing to those seeking healing for their body, the necessity of full consecration and obedience to the Lord. That afternoon I was given a card and was to be prayed for at the first divine healing service. After spending most of the day in prayer, I went to the arena that night expecting to be prayed for, but as the service progressed darkness settled down over me—a cloud through which I could not glimpse any ray of light. I felt that I could not be prayed for that night. I must first find what was this cloud between myself and my Lord.

The Clouds Roll By

"Most of that night I spent in prayer; morning found me still struggling—not yet had light dawned in my heart. At last utterly worn out with the struggle, I literally threw myself on my face and cried out to God, 'O Lord, I don't know what is the matter; if you don't show me what is standing between Thee and me, there is no hope for me, I am undone.'

"I had come to the end of myself, and then it was that the Lord could begin to talk to my heart. In that moment I fully realized my own utter insufficiency and dependence upon God. It seemed then that the Lord Himself quieted me, and, oh how tenderly, showed me my own heart, and that which was standing between the blessing I sought and myself. As though an open book had been placed before me, I saw and read my heart there. It had taken a terrible struggle. I believe I had not before been willing to have the Lord show me wherein lay the trouble, but now it was all plain. I saw it all, pride and ambition! During the few years of my life that I had been strong enough to study, I had made considerable progress in music— had been told by some of the best authorities that I could be a concert performer. I loved music with a love that was positively idolatrous. Other branches of study were intensely fascinating to me also. Whenever a little accession of strength would come, I would plunge into study with the greatest ardor only to have fondly cherished hopes and ambitions again struck down.

"As I lay quiet and still in His sacred presence, it was as though He spoke to my heart, quieting all its anxiety and pain, 'My child, if I heal you, will you give Me those things you love so well, will you yield to Me your little all?'

"I thought it over for a little, and at last made the surrender, 'Dear Lord,' I said, 'I know I have always put those things first in my life, but, Lord, from this time, if You say never touch a piano again, as long as I live I never will; if You say never open another book besides the Bible, as long as I live I never will.'

"From the depths of my heart I meant it, and God knew I meant it. Never can I tell the peace that flooded my soul in that moment of complete consecration. Peace and joy thrilled my being. Praise God! Never shall I forget that hour alone with God.

"Just when it seemed I had given up all to Him, then it was that He, in His love and tenderness, seemed to take those things and give them back to me—but there was a difference—they were His now, as well as mine, they were purified, to be used only as He would have and for His glory. To this day when I play the piano that moment comes back to me so vividly; music is sacred; it is now for His praise and glory.

Jehovah Rapha

"Well, I was having a wonderful time there alone with my Lord who was becoming with each passing moment more precious to my heart, when there came a knock at the door. It was a neighbor who, knowing that I was alone, had come to see if I was all right. I was sorry to be disturbed for I surely was having a glorious time, however, I rose and went to the door. As I opened it she looked at me and quite suddenly threw up both her hands. I wondered what could be wrong, but in a moment she exclaimed:

"'Miss Fox, what has happened?'

"'Happened?' I echoed. 'Why, what do you mean?'

"'Your eyes,' she said. 'What has happened to your eyes? Don't you know? Go, look in the mirror!'

"Needless to say, I did look, and praise the Lord, what do you think I found ? A film had been slowly forming over my eyes, dimming them. I do not know just what it was—the doctors did not seem to understand it. One specialist had told me that I would eventually be hopelessly blind. Now, as I gazed in the mirror I found that *the film had all gone from my eyes*. They were bright and clear. As yet the sight was no better, but the dim glaz[ed] look was all gone. God had given me the earnest of my healing when I surrendered my little all to Him. I prayed no more that day. I could only praise Him. *I knew He would heal me!*

"That night I went again to the arena and eagerly awaited the time when Dr. Price would pray for the sick. Sitting there amongst the sick and suffering how my heart thrilled with hope! As I listened to those God-inspired messages faith had sprung up within my heart, and now it amounted to certainty. I knew I would be healed. As I sat there I could feel the power of God; scarcely could I keep my seat.

"One thing I had determined on, however, I would not fall when I should be prayed for, no indeed, I was a dignified church member, and I would draw the line at that! I liked everything very quiet!

"But somehow when I went forward for prayer, the Lord came so near, His presence was so great and so precious, that all else was forgotten, and before I could realize what had happened I was lying on my back in the sawdust. Oh, the solemnity, the sacredness, the joy of that hour! Forgotten were the great crowds! Unmindful of the many curious eyes, I was lost to all but the joy and peace that were flooding my soul. It seemed as though I were shut away alone with my precious Lord. I was just becoming acquainted with Him in a real personal way. I found I could talk with Him there. Indeed He became in that sacred hour all in all to me. I believe I can truthfully say that that night I got beyond the desire for physical healing, got beyond the desire for mere blessing; I desired above all things else the Healer Himself. I wanted the Blesser rather than the blessing. But thank God, I found I could have both, Blesser and blessing, Healer and healing. I was shut away alone with Him. True I knew where I was, was conscious of the people around me—yet it seemed that I was alone with Him—Jesus and I! Hallelujah! He became to me in that glorious hour the Rose of Sharon, the Lily of the Valley, the Bright and Morning Star, yea, the One altogether lovely!

Sunshine at Last

"I do not know how long I lay there, but presently I arose. Then it was that the realization of a remarkable change came to me. I noticed immediately that the stiffness was gone from my knee, and the swelling was all gone from my leg. When I entered the arena that night my [leg] from my knee to my foot was badly swollen and very painful—now both swelling and pain were gone. Praise the Lord!

"I was very busy looking down at my foot; it was so wonderful to have it free from pain and stiffness. I kept looking down—it pays to look up sometimes, as I found out. When I did finally look up I found another cause for rejoicing. I could read the signs in the arena. How I rejoiced! How happy I was!

"On my way home I could scarcely contain myself. I read all the advertisements in the street car—I read all about the merits of Lux and Old Dutch Cleanser, auto tires and all sorts of things. My friends were much amused and happy. So was I! In fact I never felt happier in my life. The Lord had fulfilled His Word! I could have shouted the praises of God! However, I behaved very decorously—relieving my exuberant spirits by reading the advertisements, and enjoying to the full my new-found ability to read them.

"One thing, however, caused me to wonder. I still had pain in my stomach and abdomen. It did not frighten me, though. I knew the Lord would complete the work He had begun in my body. The pain and stiffness were gone from my limb, the fever was gone, and I had not coughed any more. I knew that all would be well!

"When I retired to my room that night, the pain still continued, and after I was in bed it became steadily worse. More and more intense it became till I wondered how I could endure it. Still I knew all would be well! I knew I was going to be completely delivered, and in the midst of the pain I kept praising God. At last there came another pain, different from any I had ever had in my life. It was sharp, hot, I cannot describe it, but as it flashed through my body, my stomach and abdomen heaved upward, something inside me snapped and loosened and I felt every organ go to its place in my body. That was the last pain I had. Praise God! I was healed!

"Shortly after my healing the Lord filled me with the Holy Spirit, and a few months later I received a call into the harvest field and have since been preaching the unsearchable riches of this Christ who is all in all to me. I know that He is the same yesterday and today and forever. I proved His Word and found it true, and praise His name, that which He has done for me He is able to do for all who read this testimony of His power to save and heal.

"I shall always thank God for the ministry of Brother Price and what it has meant to our family in the healing of myself and my brother. May the Lord continue to bless his consecrated ministry in the future as in the past to countless thousands throughout the world."

That, my friends, is the testimony of Miss Ethel Fox. It is not merely a healing...it is a miracle of the power of God.

Chapter 27

From Saint Vitus' Dance to Victory

(Lorne Fox, Vancouver, Washington)

*N*ow close your eyes again and try to visualize the splendid young man for whom the world of motion picture and radio has been bidding, but whose life belongs to Jesus. Hear him as he testifies. He is Lorne Fox, evangelist and musician, another living testimony of the power of Jesus to heal:

"It is with a heart full of gratitude and love that I write this testimony of the marvelous healing power of the Lord Jesus! At the early age of five sickness and trouble came into my life—convulsions followed by terrible bilious attacks! For hours I would lie in the dark night of unconsciousness, followed by sick headaches.

"Operations were performed on my nose and throat, doctors thinking this would help, but on the contrary, I became worse, until a couple of summers later I took stomach and intestinal flu of a very serious nature. This left me in a very weakened condition, for in those weeks of suffering the doctors had given up hope for me—but God had another plan for my life and again I rallied—but this time with an aggravated form of

Saint Vitus' dance.[1] My heart became greatly enlarged, and often troubled me to the extent that sleep or rest was impossible. Then with the Saint Vitus' dance was a continual fever. Almost constantly night and day I ran a fever.

"Doctors in various towns and cities were consulted, and finally a serum was given which caused the poison to leave my body in the form of big purplish blotches. The serum was administered hypodermically. For a few short weeks the fever left and I was better, but over-exhaustion brought the disease back again and it was worse than before.

"We went at this time to the city of Edmonton [Alberta], Canada, and doctors opened my spine at the base and drained the fluid to see if it was diseased. However, I became steadily worse, and was taken to the hospital and operated on, but with no success.

"My schooling was practically a failure as at the time of my healing I was 12 years of age and only in the third grade. I was undersized, and, of course, underweight. The disease had shattered my nerves to the extent that feeding myself was speedily becoming impossible. I was liable to put my food in one of my eyes or in my ears, or somewhere else, instead of in my mouth!

"At night my father kept his arm over me in order to keep me from jumping and jerking out onto the floor. My ankle joints had become so weak that I could scarcely walk a few steps without falling, and would lie helpless until someone picked me up. My heart had become very much enlarged and weakened. The doctors shook their heads, and tried to plan some way to find relief. Another operation was advised, but praise God, I was healed just a few days before the operation was to have been performed. The doctors got together in consultation over the case, and finally issued their ultimatum—I would not likely live to grow up, and if I did, I would always be a helpless invalid, never able to work for myself.

"But one day, in the bluest, darkest hour, a man of God, Dr. Price, came to Edmonton, and I was taken to the services. On the first Saturday night none but children were prayed for— and I was one of those children! Those standing near me as Dr. Price prayed for me said that I jumped completely off my seat, and then it was like an electric shock went through me. Thank God, that was the last jump or jerk I've ever had from that disease from that day to this.

"That was many years ago, and today I'm well and strong only through the power of the blood of Jesus, and my heart's desire is that I might be just a humble servant of His until He comes. With the poet, may I say:

'Take my life, and let it be
Consecrated, Lord, to Thee.' "

Endnote

1. Saint Vitus' dance, or chorea: "a nervous disorder marked by spasmodic movements of limbs and facial muscles and by incoordination." *Merriam Webster's Collegiate Dictionary*, Tenth Edition.

Chapter 28

Victory Just Now

*A*re you sick, my brother? Are you suffering, my sister?

Just sit down with the open Bible before you and begin to read carefully and prayerfully the Word of the Lord. Ask God to reveal it to your own heart.

If there is sin there, pray that He might cleanse you with the blood that was shed upon Calvary's cross. Nothing but the blood of Jesus can wash away sin. When faith comes to the door of your heart, it turns away if it beholds sin reigning in the life. If we allow sin to reign, then we give the devil, who is the author of disease, a grip upon us. He will fight very hard against the healing of your body.

James declares, "Confess your faults one to another that you may be healed." The confession must precede the healing. The Scriptures tell us that we have confidence toward God when our hearts condemn us not.

You cannot have healing without the Healer. It is Jesus Himself that we need. We must invite Him into a surrendered, consecrated, purified heart.

By your side is standing the compassionate Christ. In the room where you now are, be it at home or hospital, or foreign field, there is the sympathizing Jesus. Tell Him that you know He is there. Tell Him that you love Him. Tell Him you want to be healed for His glory. Tell Him that you have taken the promises and are standing upon them. Tell Him that you will go wherever He leadeth, then I am sure that that wonderful Savior—Healer of both soul and body—will become the author and finisher of your faith.

Through your weakness there will flow His strength. The faith that He alone can bring will so fill the heart that there will be no room for doubt. The arms of your Savior will be felt underneath, lifting you above your burdens and your fears.

Through your pain-racked body will flow the stream of the resurrection life of our risen Lord. You will be so overwhelmed by the glory of His presence, that for a while your physical powers will weaken under the strength of the spiritual blessing. Rest assured you will come out from under the touch of His hand with a testimony that you will be able to give to the world that Jesus saves and Jesus heals.

Ministries of CARVER and ENLOE

JOHN CARVER serves the body of Christ as pastor, evangelist, educator, and historian. He is recognized as an authority on modern Pentecostal history, specializing in the divine healing movement. His Faith Outreach Archives preserves rare historical materials to fulfill his passion of mentoring young ministers in the ministry of signs and wonders.

For more ministry information, visit their website:
www.johncarverministries.org

TIM ENLOE is a teacher-evangelist and a student of Pentecostal and Charismatic church history. His conference on the Holy Spirit ministry impacts churches with the Spirit's baptizing, healing, and transforming power. His presentations on Pentecostal Revival History stir believers to recapture their New Testament inheritance.

For more ministry information, visit their website:
www.enloeministries.org

Additional copies of this book and other
book titles from DESTINY IMAGE are
available at your local bookstore.

For a complete list of our titles,
visit us at www.destinyimage.com
Send a request for a catalog to:

Destiny Image® Publishers, Inc.

P.O. Box 310
Shippensburg, PA 17257-0310

*"Speaking to the Purposes of God for This
Generation and for the Generations to Come"*